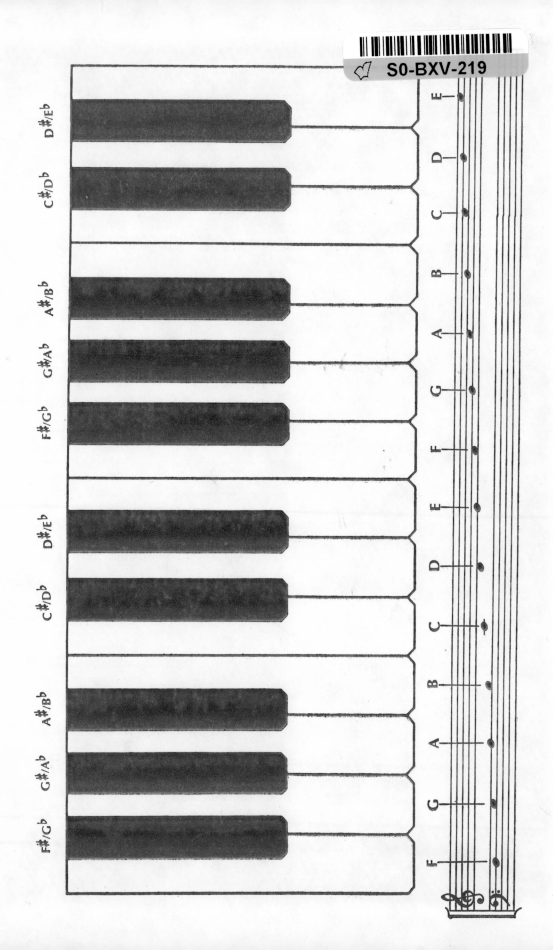

World of Music

MARY PALMER • **MARY LOUISE REILLY**
CAROL ROGEL SCOTT
Authors

CARMINO RAVOSA
Theme Musical

JILL TRINKA
Reading Music

DARRELL BLEDSOE
Producer, Vocal Recordings

PHYLLIS WEIKART
Rhythmic Competency

Silver Burdett & Ginn

Morristown, NJ • Needham, MA
Atlanta, GA • Cincinnati, OH • Dallas, TX • Deerfield, IL • Menlo Park, CA

CONTENTS

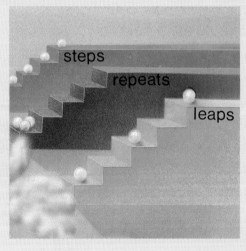

steps

repeats

leaps

SECTION I
MUSIC FOR LIVING

HELLO, EV'RYBODY!

Listen to this song.

Sometimes a word is left out.
Sing a friend's name in place
of it.

Ev'rybody's Welcome

Folk Song from Tennessee

Ev - 'ry-bod - y's wel - come,— yes, yes, wel - come!

Ev - 'ry-bod - y's wel - come,— come a-long and go.

Oh, glo - ry, hal - le - lu - jah!

Oh, glo - ry, come a-long and go.

From *SONGS OF THE OLD CAMP GROUND,* compiled by L. L. McDowell. Reprinted by permission.

4 ◁UNIT 1▷ **Music from Day to Day**

A WALKING SONG

Have you ever rambled about, not really going anywhere?

This person likes to go rambling.

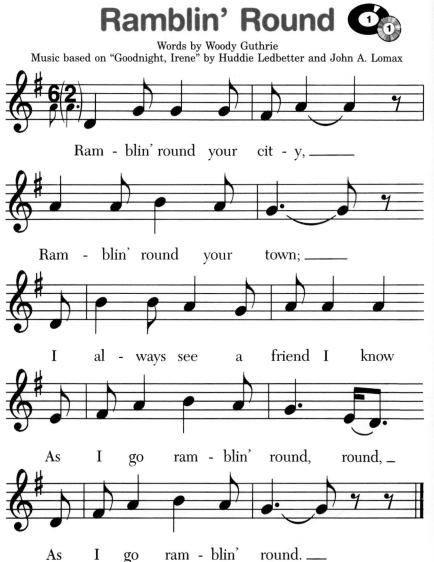

Ramblin' Round

Words by Woody Guthrie
Music based on "Goodnight, Irene" by Huddie Ledbetter and John A. Lomax

Ram - blin' round your cit - y, _____

Ram - blin' round your town; _____

I al - ways see a friend I know

As I go ram - blin' round, round, _

As I go ram - blin' round. _____

A Special Person

Why is the person in this song called Bongo Joe?

What makes him special?

bongos

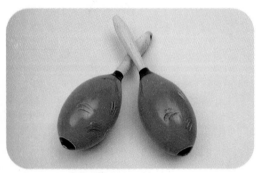

maracas

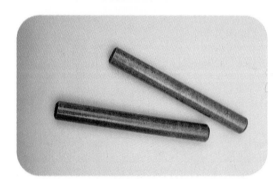

claves

Bongo Joe

Words and Music by Judy Rector Rodger

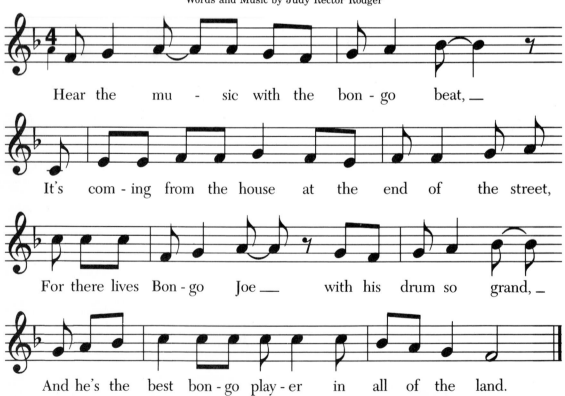

Hear the music with the bon-go beat, —

It's com-ing from the house at the end of the street,

For there lives Bon-go Joe — with his drum so grand, —

And he's the best bon-go play-er in all of the land.

A HAPPY SONG

Think of a happy way to look
as you sing.
Think of a happy way to move.

Little Wheel A-Turnin'

African-American Spiritual

1. There's a lit-tle wheel a-turn-in' in my heart,

There's a lit-tle wheel a-turn-in' in my heart;

In my heart, _____ in my heart. _____

There's a lit-tle wheel a-turn-in' in my heart.

2. There's a little song a-singin' in my heart,

3. There's a little love a-livin' in my heart,

4. There's a little bell a-ringin' in my heart,

5. There's a little drum a-beatin' in my heart,

Let's Celebrate!

Everybody has a birthday.
When is yours?

How Old Are You?

Folk Song from Texas

All

"How — old are you, my pret-ty lit-tle miss?
fine — lit-tle lad?

How — old are you, my hon-ey?"

She —
He — an-swered me with a tee hee hee,

Birthday Child

"I'll be eight-years-old on Sun-day."

All

The yad - dle lad - dle lad - dle um dai - sy,

The yad - dle lad - dle lad - dle um, Yad - dle lad - dle lad - dle um,

Yad - dle lad - dle lad - dle um dai - sy.

A VISIT TO THE OCEAN

Pretend that you are a scuba diver.

What do you see
on the ocean floor?
A clam? A big fish?
An octopus?

In the Sea

Words and Music by Lynn Olson

Div - ing to a wa - ter - y trip In the sea,

That can be a dan - ger - ous dip In the sea!

Rest - less waves a - bove you, O - cean floor be - low you—

Search - ing through a shad - ow - y world In the Sea.

Act out what you hear in this music.

"Sailing" from *Harbor Vignettes* ......
.... Donaldson

ON A FARM

This song is about a farm.

Can you sing the animal names in Spanish?

el patito

el perrito

el pollito

el chanchito

el gatito

el burrito

My Farm

Folk Song from Argentina

1. I have a lit - tle farm be - side a wind - ing stream,

I have a lit - tle barn - yard where the grass is green.

El   po - lli - to   goes like   this: peep, peep,

El   po - lli - to   goes like   this: peep, peep,

O   va,   ca - ma - ra - da,   va,   ca - ma - ra - da,

Va,   O   va,   O   va;

O   va,   ca - ma - ra - da,   va,   ca - ma - ra - da,

Va,   O   va,   O   va.

2. *El patito* goes like this: quack, quack.

3. *El burrito* goes like this: hee haw.

4. *El chanchito* goes like this: oink, oink.

5. *El perrito* goes like this: woof, woof.

6. *El gatito* goes like this: meow, meow.

AT THE CIRCUS

Here comes the circus band, leading the parade.

Circus Parade

Words and Music by Milton Kaye

1. Oh, here comes the cir - cus band,

Ta - ra - ra - ra, ta - ra - ra - ra - ra,

Here comes the cir - cus band,

Ta - ra - ra - ra - ra - ra!

REFRAIN

Zing! Zing!_____ Zing! Zing!_____

Ta - ra - ra - ra, Ta - ra - ra - ra.

Oh, how much I love the cir - cus, Ta - ra - ra! Boom! Boom!

2. Oh, here come the elephants,
   Clump-clump-ta-ra, clump-clump-ta-ra-ra,
   Here come the elephants,
   Clump-clump-ta-ra-ra-ra. *Refrain*

3. Oh, here come the merry clowns,
   Ha-ha-ta-ra, ha-ha-ta-ra-ra,
   Here come the merry clowns,
   Ha-ha-ta-ra-ra-ra. *Refrain*

4. Oh, here come the dancing bears,
   Thump-thump-ta-ra, thump-thump-ta-ra-ra,
   Here come the dancing bears,
   Thump-thump-ta-ra-ra-ra. *Refrain*

In *The Red Pony* a boy dreams about a circus.
Listen to the music that the circus band plays.

"Circus Music" from *The Red Pony*
. . . . Copland

BAREBACK RIDERS　　　　　　　　　　　　　　　*W. H. Brown*

W.H. Brown, *Bareback Riders*,
National Gallery of Art, Gift of Edgar William and Bernice Chrysler Garbisch, Washington, D.C.

A NONSENSE SONG

Five of the letters in this song are vowels.
Which letter is not a vowel?

B-A, Bay
American Folk Song

B - A, bay, B - E, bee, B - I, bid-die by, B - O, bo,

Bid-die by bo, B - U, bu, Bid-die by bo bu, bu.

This is just a sil - ly song! The words don't mean a thing.

Nev - er mind the sil - ly words, Just o - pen up and sing. Oh!

B - A, bay, B - E, bee, B - I, bid-die by, B - O, bo,

Bid-die by bo, B - U, bu, Bid-die by bo bu, bu.

Courtesy of Prentice-Hall, Inc.

THE LIFE OF A COWHAND

In this song a cowhand tells about life on the trail.

Lone Star Trail

American Cowboy Song

1. I start-ed on the trail on June twen-ty-third,
I been punch-in'* Tex-as cat-tle on the Lone Star Trail;

REFRAIN
Sing-in' Ki yi yip-pi yip-pi yay, yip-pi yay!

Sing-in' Ki yi yip-pi yip-pi yay!

2. I'm up in the mornin' before daylight,
And before I sleep the moon shines bright. *Refrain*

3. Oh it's bacon and beans 'most every day,
I'd as soon be a-eatin' prairie hay. *Refrain*

4. My feet are in the stirrups and my rope is on the side,
Show me a horse that I can't ride. *Refrain*

A STORY SONG

This song tells a story about a frog and a mouse.

What other characters are in the story?

Mister Frog Went A-Courtin'

American Folk Song

1. Mis-ter Frog went a-court-in' and he did ride, Um-hm! Um-hm!

Mis-ter Frog went a-court-in' and he did ride,

Sword and pis-tol by his side, Um-hm! Um-hm!

2. He said, "Miss Mouse, are you within?"
   "Oh yes, Sir, here I sit and spin."

3. He took Miss Mouse upon his knee,
   And he said, "Miss Mouse, will you marry me?"

4. Oh, where will the wedding supper be?
   Away down yonder in a hollow tree.

5. Now Mister Frog was dressed in green,
And Miss Mouse looked like a queen.

6. The first came in was a little white moth,
He spread out the tablecloth.

7. The next came in was a bumblebee,
With a fiddle on his knee.

8. The next came in was a little flea,
To take a jig with the bumblebee.

9. The next came in was a pesky old fly,
He ate up the wedding pie.

10. The next came in was a little red ant,
She always says, "I can't, I can't."

11. The next came in was a fluffy yellow chick,
He ate so much it made him sick.

12. The next came in was an old tomcat,
He swallowed Miss Mouse as quick as a rat.

13. Then gentleman Frog swam over the lake,
But he got swallowed by a big fat snake.

14. There's bread and cheese upon the shelf,
If you want any more you can sing it yourself.

Move to this music as Mister Frog and Miss Mouse might move.

"Walking Song" from *Acadian Songs and Dances* . . . . **Thomson**

I'M SPECIAL!

It's me!
It's something to shout about!
It's great to be nobody else but me!

It's Me!

Words and Music by Carmino Ravosa

REFRAIN

It's me! No-bod-y else but me!

It's me! There's no one I'd rath-er be.

VERSE

1. Long or short or thin or fat,
   oh, what do I care,
   When I look in the mirror just so
   long as I'm there? *Refrain*

2. Smart or dumb or weak or tough,
   there's nothing to fear
   As long as when I call myself
   I answer "Here!" *Refrain*

3. Black or white, I don't care 'bout
   the color of my skin
   As long as I've got sump'n to keep
   my insides in. *Last Refrain*

LAST REFRAIN

It's me! No-bod-y else but me!

It's me! There's no one I'd rath-er be.

It's me, it's me, it's me, it's me, it's me!

COME, RIDE THE TRAIN!

Same Train

African-American Folk Melody   Words by Holsaert-Bailey

1. Same train __ a - blow - in' at the sta - tion,

Same train, __ same train. __

Same train __ wait - in' for the peo - ple,

Same train, __ same train. __

Same train __ leav - in' the sta - tion,

Same train __ be back to - mor - row,

Same train, _ same train. __

2. Same train a-comin' down the line,
   Same train, same train.
   Same train pickin' up speed,
   Same train, same train.
   Same train goin' like sixty,
   Same train be back tomorrow,
   Same train, same train.

3. Same train a-chuggin' up the mountain,⎫
   Hard pull, hard pull.   ⎬ 2 *times*
   Same train easy down the mountain,
   Same train be back tomorrow, . . .

4. Same train a-passin' all the farmyards,⎫
   Same train, same train.   ⎬ 2 *times*
   Same train a-passin' all the farmyards,
   Same train be back tomorrow, . . .

5. Same train a-whistlin' at the crossroads,⎫
   Same train, same train.   ⎬ 2 *times*
   Same train a-whistlin' at the crossroads,
   Same train be back tomorrow, . . .

6. Same train a-comin' to the tunnel, . . .
   Same train a-speedin' through the tunnel, . . .
   Same train out in the sunlight,
   Same train be back tomorrow, . . .

7. Same train a-blowin' for the station, . . .
   Same train a-stoppin' at the station, . . .
   Same train a-droppin' all the people,
   Same train be back tomorrow, . . .

Listen to this music about a train.

LISTENING LIBRARY

"The Little Train of the Caipira" from
Bachianas Brasileiras No. 2 . . . . . . Villa-Lobos

There's Work to Be Done!

Do you ever sing when you work or play?
Singing helps to make a task a little easier.

Cotton Needs Pickin'

Southern Work Song

A REFRAIN

Cot - ton needs pick - in' so _____ bad, ___

Cot - ton needs pick - in' so bad, ___

Cot - ton needs pick - in' so bad,

Fine

I'm gon - na pick all o - ver this field.

B VERSE

Plant - ed this cot - ton in A - pril

On the full of the moon,

We've had a hot dry sum - mer,

D.C. al Fine

And that's why it o-pened so soon, Oh,

A SONG JUST FOR YOU

What seasons are mentioned in the poem?
What seasons are mentioned in the song?

Sing a Song of Seasons

Sing a song of seasons!
Something bright in all!
Flowers in the summer,
Fires in the fall.

Robert Louis Stevenson

The Circle of Seasons

Words and Music by Carmino Ravosa

REFRAIN

The circle of seasons, The circle of seasons,

Around and around they go.

} *2 times*

VERSE

1. Wheth-er you ski, fly a kite, toss a ball,

D.C.

De-pends up-on win-ter, spring, sum-mer, and fall.

2. The food that you eat,
   What you wear on your feet—
   That all depends on the
   sun and the heat. *Refrain*

3. The way that you dress,
   With more or with less,
   Depends on the season
   and on your address. *Refrain*

© 1984 Carmino Ravosa

Meet the Composer

The man in the picture is Carmino Ravosa (kahr MEE noh rah VOH sah). He wrote "The Circle of Seasons." He likes to write songs for boys and girls like you. Listen to the recording to hear him tell about his music.

Carmino Ravosa
(1930–   )

Listening to the Composer

IN THE HALL OF THE MOUNTAIN KING

There is a terrible fuss at the palace!
The trolls can hear the noise, even in
their faraway cave.

Travel with the trolls from the cave
to the palace.

"In the Hall of the Mountain King" from
Peer Gynt Suite No. 1 . . . . Grieg

About the Music

In Norway, children learn about Peer Gynt (pehr ghihnt). Peer was a young man who had many adventures. One of them took place among some nasty trolls.

The composer Edvard Grieg (EHD vahrd greeg) wrote music for the story of Peer Gynt. You will hear the music for Peer's troll adventure. It is called "In the Hall of the Mountain King." Your teacher will tell you the story. Then listen to the recording. Hear how the music catches the spirit of Peer's adventure.

COUNTING THE STARS

Twinkle, twinkle, little star,
How I wonder what you are!

Have you ever seen the night sky
filled with twinkling stars?
Did it make you wonder?
Did it make you dream?

Star Song

Folk Song from Austria

I count-ed in the heav-en, Where the moon shed its light,

White stars that num-bered sev-en, They were twin-kling so bright.

REFRAIN

I count-ed one, I count-ed two, I count-ed three,

I count-ed four, I count-ed five, I count-ed six,

I count-ed sev'n, Good night.

MORE COUNTING

Children in Mexico use Spanish words to count from one to ten.
Listen for their counting words in this song.

Counting Song

Children's Song from Mexico   Words by Lucille Wood

1. U - no, dos, y tres, Cua - tro, cin - co, seis;

Sie - te, o - cho, nue - ve, I can count to diez.

REFRAIN

La la la la la, La la la la la, La la la la la la;

La la la la la, La la la la la, La la la la la la.

2. Tengo un sombrero,

   I have a little hat;

   Tengo un sarape,

   What do you think of that? *Refrain*

3. Adios, amigo,

   Adios, my friend;

   Hasta la vista,

   Till we meet again. *Refrain*

CHITTER, CHATTER

When you chatter, you talk with someone.

Imagine talking with an angel!

Chatter with the Angels

African-American Folk Song

Chat - ter with the an - gels soon in the morn - in',

Chat - ter with the an - gels in that land!

Chat - ter with the an - gels soon in the morn - in',

Chat - ter with the an - gels, Join that band!

I hope to join that band

And chat-ter with the an - gels all day long!

I hope to join that band

And chat-ter with the an - gels all day long!

A SINGING GAME

These happy workers sing
about their good life.
They call it *la buena,
buena vida*.

San Severino

Folk Song from Chile

1. San Se - ve - ri - no, la bue - na, bue - na vi - da;

San Se - ve - ri - no, la bue - na, bue - na vi - da.

Now this way and now that, so goes *el car - pin - te - ro*

A - *sí,* a - *sí,* a - *sí,* this is the life for me.

2. Now this way and now that, so goes *el zapatero.*

3. Now this way and now that, so goes *el panadero.*

4. Now this way and now that, so goes *el caballero.*

Play this pattern on claves each time you hear it.

Now this way and now that

A LULLABY

In this song a mother is singing her child to sleep.

She calls the child by a special name. What is it?

Sleep, My Little Bird

Yiddish Folk Song   English Version by Holsaert-Bailey

Sleep, my lit - tle bird,   Close your drow - sy eyes,

Eye — lu — lu — lu.

Rest in health, my child,   Un - der peace - ful skies,

Eye — lu — lu — lu.

From SING A SONG by Charity Bailey; © 1955 Plymouth Music Co., Inc.

Moth-er's al-ways near, So you need not fear,

Eye — lu — lu — lu.

Sleep and have sweet dreams, While you're young, life seems

Full of light and love, Eye — lu lu lu.

Lullaby, Oh, Lullaby!

Lullaby, oh, lullaby!
Flowers are closed and lambs are sleeping;
Lullaby, oh, lullaby!
Stars are up, the moon is peeping;
Lullaby, oh, lullaby!
While the birds are silence keeping,
(Lullaby, oh, lullaby!)
Sleep, my baby, fall a-sleeping,
Lullaby, oh, lullaby!

Christina Rossetti

SING! WHISTLE! HUM!

Your mouth and voice can make different kinds of sounds.

It can sing.

It can hum.

It can whistle.

Use your mouth all three ways in this song.

Whistle While You Work

Words and Music by Larry Morey and Frank Churchill

Just whis-tle while you work. (Whistle.) _____

Put on that grin and start right in to whis-tle loud and long.

Just hum a mer-ry tune. *(Hum.)* _____

Just do your best, then take a rest and sing your-self a song.

When there's too much to do, Don't let it both-er you.

For - get your trou - ble, try to be

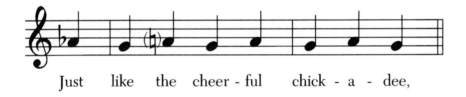

Just like the cheer - ful chick - a - dee,

And whis - tle while you work. *(Whistle.)* _____

Come on, get smart, tune up and start to whis-tle while you work.

A Visit to Hawaii

In Hawaii, dancers tell this rainbow story
with their hands.

What hand motion would you use to show
a rainbow?

Hawaiian Rainbows

Folk Song from Hawaii

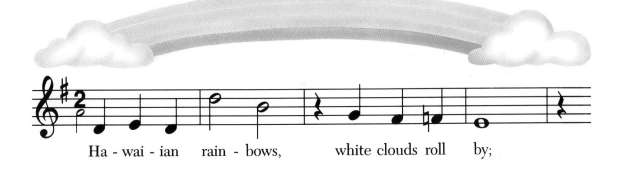

Ha - wai - ian rain - bows, white clouds roll by;

You show your col - ors a - gainst the sky.

Ha - wai - ian rain - bows, it seems to me,

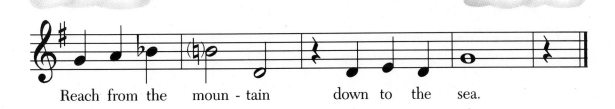

Reach from the moun - tain down to the sea.

It's Fiesta Time!

Listen for the tambourine and castanets.

tambourine

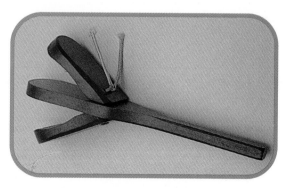

castanets

La raspa

Folk Song from Mexico   English Version by Rosemary Jacques

Now work of the day is done, And un-der the set-ting sun,

The mu-sic calls ev-'ry-one To come and join in the fun.

Their voic-es are sing-ing a hap-py song,

No-bod-y has a care;

And peo - ple are glad that the night is long,

Laugh-ter is ev - 'ry - where.

LET'S RIDE ON THE WATER!

How do boats move?
Show their motion as you sing.

Come Sailing with Me

Folk Song from Italy

1. Come   sail - ing   with   me, _____

Come   sail - ing   with   me; _____

Float-ing   a - long,   oh   how   hap - py   we'll   be,

Come sail - ing with me. _____

2. Come rowing with me,
   Come rowing with me;
   Pulling the oars, oh how
      happy we'll be,
   Come rowing with me.

3. Come boating with me,
   Come boating with me;
   Zooming along, oh how
      happy we'll be,
   Come boating with me.

This painting shows boats called *gondolas*.
Imagine riding in one of them!

THE RIALTO BRIDGE   *Francesco Guardi*

Picture yourself in a gondola as you listen
to this music.

"Barcarolle" from *Tales of Hoffmann*
. . . . **Offenbach**

A SAFETY LESSON

The boy and girl in this song live in Trinidad. They sing about the same things you do.

Their mother teaches them how to keep safe. What does she tell them to do?

Growing-Up Song

Calypso from Trinidad

REFRAIN

I am a lit-tle boy/girl from Tri - ni - dad, __

Some - times I am good, some - times I am bad.

Ma - ma she talk, talk all the day __

How I should grow up and how I should play.

VERSE

Keep out of fire, — you will get burned, —

Keep out of fire, — you will get burned; —

I don't be-lieve her, — try to de-ceive her, —

No more play with fire — I have learned.

By the Sea

Some children live near the ocean.
They see sea gulls that fly over the waves.

Can you hear the music in this song moving
upward and downward, like a sea gull's wings?

Three White Gulls

Folk Song from Italy   English Words by Marguerite Wilkinson

1. There are three — white gulls — a - fly - ing;

There are three — white gulls — a - fly - ing;

There are three — white gulls a - fly - ing; —

By the sea they cry, By the sea they cry, By the sea they cry.

"The Three Doves" from BOTSFORD COLLECTION OF FOLKSONGS, Volume 3, © 1921, 1922 G. Schirmer, Inc. Used by permission.

There are three — white gulls a - fly - ing; —

By the sea they cry, By the sea they cry, By the sea they cry.

2. In the waves they dip their soft wings;
    In the waves they dip their soft wings;
    In the waves they dip their soft wings;
    Then soar to the sky,
    Then soar to the sky,
    Then soar to the sky.
    In the waves they dip their soft wings;
    Then soar to the sky,
    Then soar to the sky,
    Then soar to the sky.

AQUARIUM

Listen to this music. Can you hear sounds that suggest beautiful, shiny fish?

"Aquarium" from *Carnival of the Animals*............Saint-Saëns

These fish show the shape of the first phrase of "Aquarium."

This is how the phrase looks in music notes.

These lines also show the shape of phrases in "Aquarium."
How are the sets of lines different from each other?

1. —　　—　—　—　—
　　　　　—　　—　　—
　　　　　　　　　　　—
　　　　　　　　　　　　　　—
　　　　　　　　　　　—

2. —　　—　—

About the Music

Music cannot really paint pictures or tell a story. But sometimes, music helps us imagine a picture or a story. The music of "Aquarium" has a calm feeling. It helps us imagine a quiet "fishy" world.

"Aquarium" is part of a long piece of music called *Carnival of the Animals*. It was written by the composer Camille Saint-Saëns (kah meel san sahn). *Carnival of the Animals* has many sections. Each one is about a different animal.

A STORY SONG

This song tells about
Noah, an ark, and animals.

Listen for the story.

Who Built the Ark?

REFRAIN

African-American Spiritual

Who built the ark? No - ah, No - ah,

Fine

Who built the ark? Broth-er No - ah built the ark.

VERSE

1. Now did - n't old No - ah build the ark? —

After each four verses D.C.

He built it out of a hick - o - ry bark, — 2. He

2. (He) built it long, both wide and tall,
   Plenty of room for the large and small,

3. Now in come the animals two by two,
   Hippopotamus and kangaroo,

4. Now in come the animals three by three,
   Two big cats and a bumble bee. *Refrain*

5. Now in come the animals four by four,
   Two through the window and two through the door,

6. Now in come the animals five by five,
   Four little sparrows and the redbird's wife,

7. Now in come the animals six by six,
   Elephant laughed at the monkey's tricks,

8. Now in come the animals seven by seven,
   Four from home and the rest from heaven. *Refrain*

9. Now in come the animals eight by eight,
   Some were on time and the others were late,

10. Now in come the animals nine by nine,
    Some was a-shouting and some was a-crying.

11. Now in come the animals ten by ten,
    Five black roosters and five black hens,

12. Now Noah says, "Go shut that door,
    The rain's started dropping and we can't take more." *Refrain*

5–4–3–2–1–BLAST OFF!

Do you ever dream about walking on the moon?

The child in this song does.

Mission Control

Words and Music by Carmino Ravosa

Mis-sion Con-trol, — do you read me?

Will you please save — me a place?

Mis-sion Con-trol, — do you need me

On the next rock-et in space?

1. May-be I'm small, — but I'm grow-ing.

Watch, and one day — you will see.

Space is wide o - pen and wait - ing for me. _____

So, Mis - sion Con - trol, __ do you read me?

I real - ly don't take __ too much room.

Mis - sion Con - trol, __ do you need me

Last time, to Ending

On the next trip to the moon?

2. I want to study the planets.
   I want to study the stars.
   I want to go up to Venus, or Mars.
   So, Mission Control . . .

3. I'm working hard, and I'm certain
   An astronaut's what I will be.
   The sky is the limit for someone like me.
   So, Mission Control . . .

Ending (spoken):
   Mission Control, do you read me?
   I'll be seeing you in about twenty years.
   Until then, over and out.

TEST 1

Look at the song on page 10 in your book.
Find the color boxes.

Which fish below show how the notes
move in each color box on page 10?

On your worksheet, circle the fish that
show your answers.

1. Yellow Color Boxes

2. Blue Color Boxes

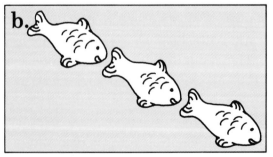

TEST 2

Choose the instrument that fits best with
each of these songs.
Circle your answers on your worksheet.

1. Lone Star Trail

2. Sleep, My Little Bird

3. Same Train

4. Bongo Joe

5. Counting Song

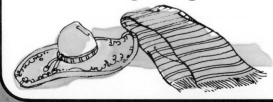  

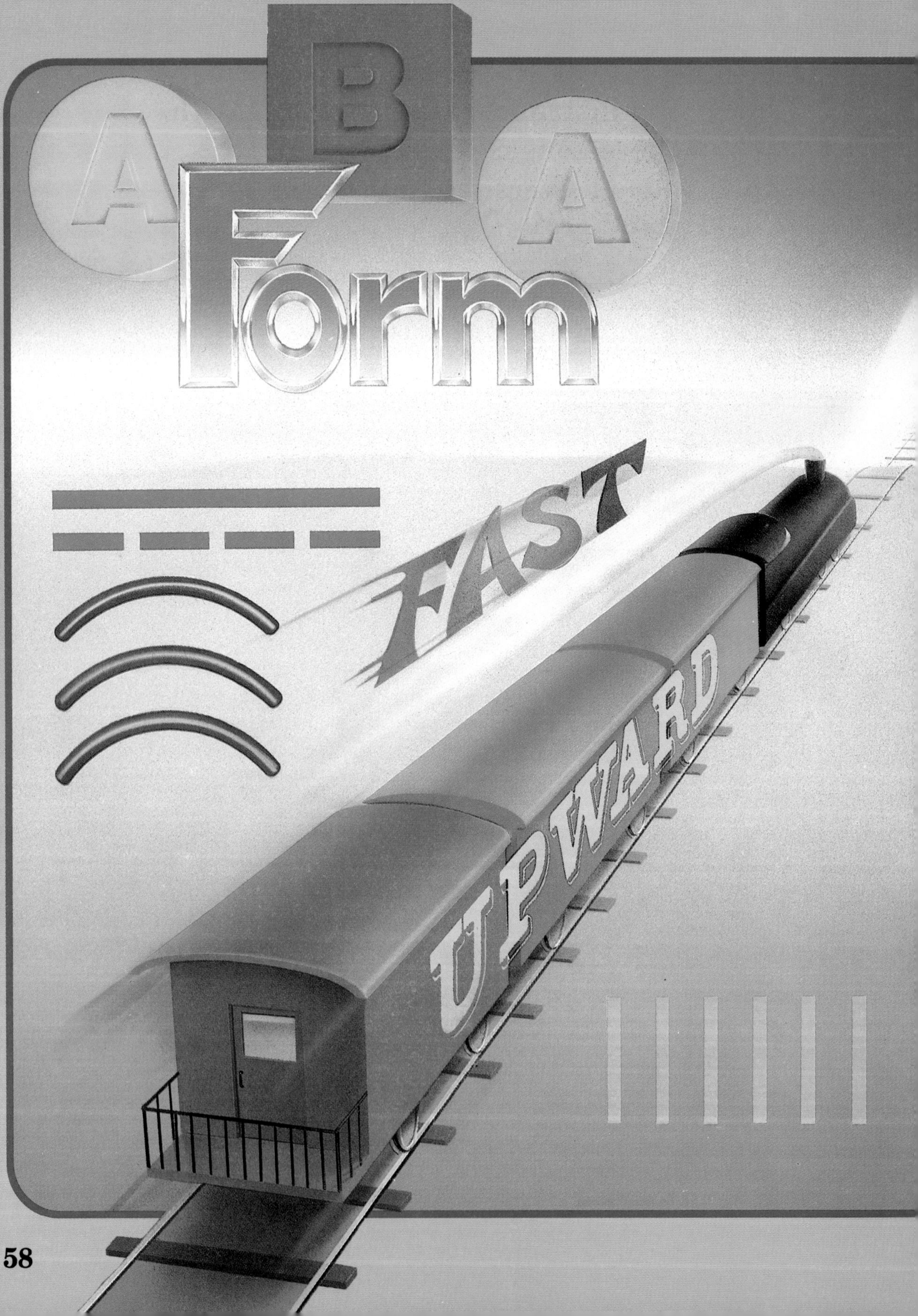
A
B
A
Form
FAST
UPWARD

SECTION II
UNDERSTANDING MUSIC

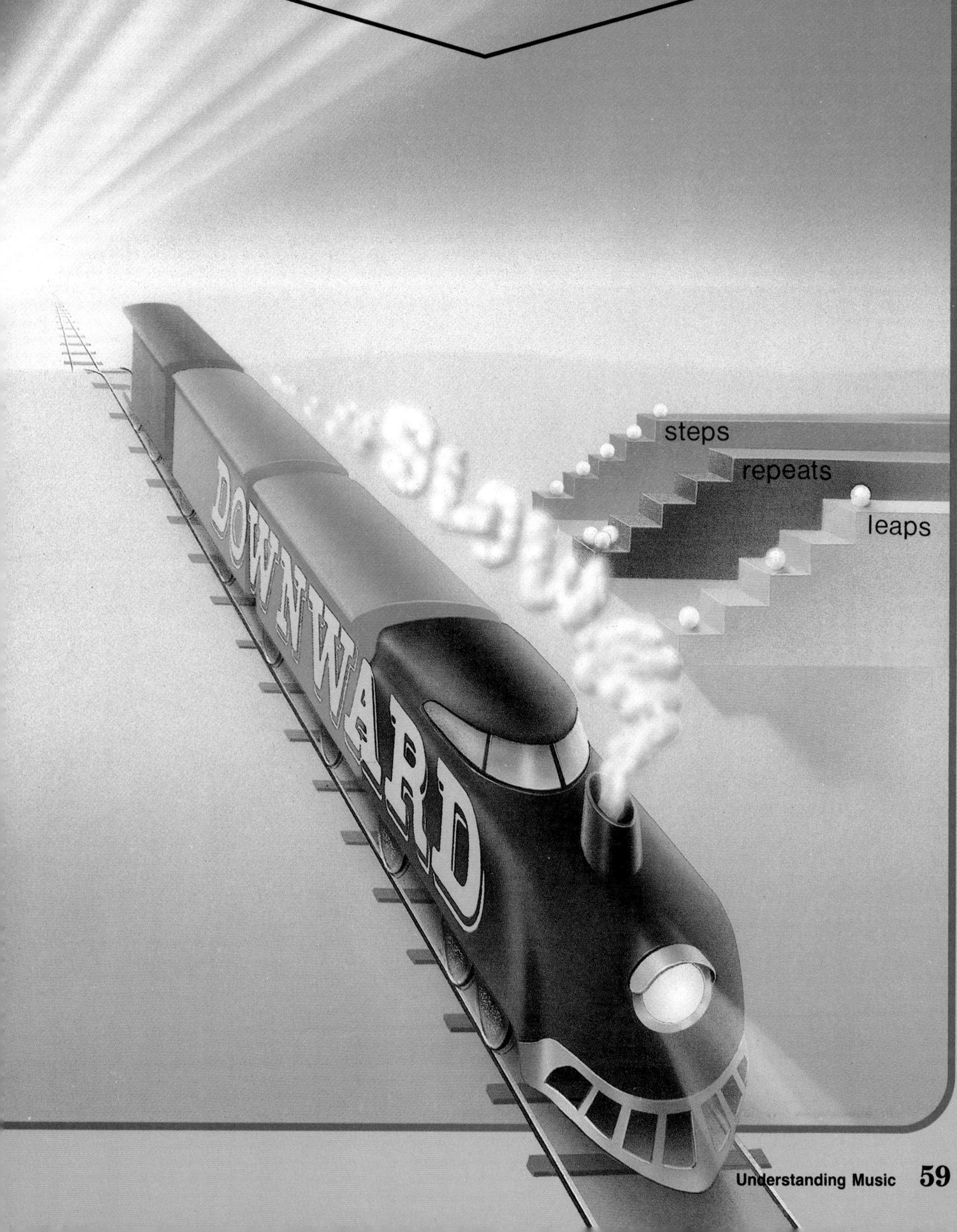

SOUNDS AROUND US

Look at the pictures.

Imagine that they can make sounds.
Describe the sounds you "hear."
Use the words below to help you.

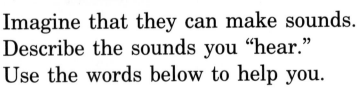

MUSIC AROUND US

Listen to the music on the recording.

Point to the word that matches the sounds you hear.

high   low   fast   slow

loud   soft   long   short

Keep the Beat

Listen for the nonsense words in this song.

Waddaly Atcha

Words and Music by Kassel-Stitzel

Wad - da - ly a - tcha, wad - da - ly a - tcha,

Doo - dle - ee - doo, _ doo - dle - ee - doo; _

Wad - da - ly a - tcha, wad - da - ly a - tcha,

Doo - dle - ee - doo, _ doo - dle - ee - doo. _

It's the sim - pl - est thing, _ noth - in' much to _ it, _

All you got to do is doo - dle - ee - doo it; _

I like the rest, — But the part I love best, —

It goes doo-dle-ee, doo-dle-ee-doo. Whoo!

You can do a hand-jive with "Waddaly Atcha."
Here are the motions.

BOUNCE AND CATCH

Show the beat by bouncing and catching a ball.

One, Two, Three, Alary

Playground Chant

1. One, two, three, a - lar - y,

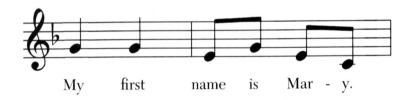

My first name is Mar - y.

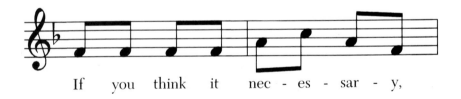

If you think it nec - es - sar - y,

Look it up in the dic - tion - ar - y.

2. One, two, three, alary,
   I saw Peter Terry
   Sitting on a bumbleberry,
   Eating lots of delicious
   cherries.

3. One, two, three, alary,
   Lost my new canary.
   When you find him,
   call him Barry.
   One, two, three, alary.

From *Sally Go Round the Sun* by Edith Fowke. Reprinted by permission of the author.

Bounce your ball to this pattern.

Listen to this music.
Try to picture the ball in motion.

"The Ball" from *Children's Games*
............................Bizet

LET'S PRETEND!

Rabbit

Folk Song from Japan

Oh,   Rab - bit,   jump - ing   free,

Tell   me, Rab - bit,   what you   see.

"When I   look   up   in - to the sky, ___

Moon is there; here __ am   I." _____

Play steady beats on a woodblock.
Follow these notes as you play.

A SPACE ADVENTURE

Imagine that you are an astronaut on the moon.

Now listen to the recording.

 ***Moon Music*** . . . . Williams

When you hear a steady beat, pretend to walk on the moon.

When you hear no beat, pretend to float in space.

FAST OR SLOW?

How would you climb a mountain?
How would you come down a mountain?
How would you go around a mountain?

We're Going Round the Mountain

Folk Song from Mississippi

1. We're go - ing round the moun - tain, two by two,

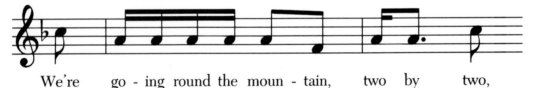

We're go - ing round the moun - tain, two by two,

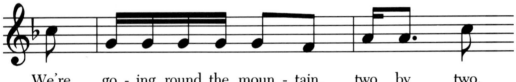

We're go - ing round the moun - tain, two by two,

So rise, Sal - ly, rise.

2. Let me see you make a
   motion, two by two, . . .

3. That's a very fine
   motion, two by two, . . .

Play steady beats on
bells while others sing.

High C

Low C

RACING AND RESTING

Look at the song title.
Will you sing this song fast or slow?

Race You down the Mountain

Words and Music by Woody Guthrie and Marjorie Mazia

1. I'll race you down the moun-tain,

I'll race you down the moun-tain,

I'll race you down the moun-tain,

We'll see who gets there first.

2. Let's run and jump the river, *(3 times)*
   We'll see who gets there first.

3. I hear myself a-huffin',
   A-huffin' and a-puffin',
   I hear myself a-huffin',
   We'll see who gets there first.

4. We'll rest beside the water, *(3 times)*
   We'll see who gets there first.

A FAST-AND-SLOW GAME

Children in Africa do a hand-pat with
this song.

Try to learn the motions from the pictures.

Kee-Chee

Game from Zaire

Ah   wu - ne ku - ne cha   o   wu - ni,

Ah   wu - ne ku - ne cha   o   wu - ni;

Ah   yi   yi   yi - ki   ay   kae   ay - na,

Ah   yi   yi   yi - ki   ay   kae   ay - na;

A   ooo _____ ah dee mee kee - chee.

1.

2.

3.

4.

STRING SOUNDS

String instruments make many different sounds.

Listen.
Then describe the sounds that you hear.

1. violin

2. autoharp

3. koto

5. dulcimer

4. musical bow

WORKING WITH STRING SOUNDS

Pluck a rubber band.
How does it sound?

Try to make the sound louder.
Here is one idea.

You can make a *diddley bow*.

Try to play the diddley
bow as shown here.

Listen to the sound of a diddley bow.

Diddley Bow Music

STYLES IN MUSIC

Pretend to play the guitar
in two different ways.

Which has the strongest
beat?

Rock About My Saro Jane

American Folk Song

Oh, rock a-bout my Sa - ro ___ Jane, ___

Oh, rock a-bout my Sa - ro Jane, ___

Oh, there's noth-ing to do but sit down and sing

And rock a-bout my Sa - ro Jane. ___

From SOMETHING TO SING ABOUT! Collected and arranged by Milton Okun. Copyright © 1968 by Milton Okun. Reprinted by permission of Macmillan Publishing Company.

REPEATED TONES

This song tells of a place where the soil
is sandy.
What crop do the people grow there?

Sandy Land

Folk Song from Oklahoma

1. Make my liv - in' in sand - y land,

Make my liv - in' in sand - y land,

Make my liv - in' in sand - y land,

La - dies, fare you well.

2. Raise sweet potatoes in sandy land, (*3 times*)
   Ladies, fare you well.

3. Dig sweet potatoes in sandy land, (*3 times*)
   Ladies, fare you well.

From THE AMERICAN PLAY PARTY SONG by B. A. Botkin. Copyright © 1937, 1963 by B. A. Botkin. Reprinted by permission of Curtis Brown, Ltd.

Play an introduction to the song.

Follow these notes.

STEPPING TONES

Children in France sing about
bells that ring in the morning.
These bells help to wake up
the town.

Do the bells wake up everyone?
Listen to find out.

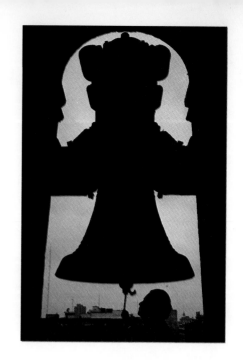

Are You Sleeping?

Folk Song from France

Are   you   sleep - ing,   Are   you   sleep - ing,

Broth - er   John,   Broth - er   John?

Morn - ing bells are ring - ing, Morn - ing bells are ring - ing,

Ding, ding, dong,   Ding, ding, dong.

Play this bell part with the song.

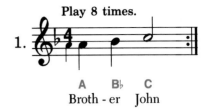

1.
Play 8 times.
A   B♭   C
Broth - er John

Listen to this music.

Pretend that you are a bell ringer.

LISTENING LIBRARY

"Grazioso" from *English Dances*
. . . .**Arnold**

Add this pattern on the bells.

D   E

PATTERNS OF STEPS

Do-Re-Mi

From THE SOUND OF MUSIC
Music by Richard Rodgers   Words by Oscar Hammerstein II

VERSE
Ⓐ
Solo

Let's start at the ver-y be-gin-ning! ___

A ver-y good place to start. ___

When you read you be-gin with A, B, C,

When you sing you be-gin with do-re-mi.

Chorus   *Solo*

Do-re-mi?   Do-re-mi.

The first three notes just hap-pen to be

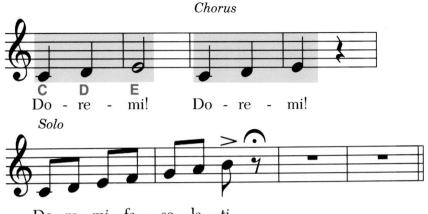

Chorus

C D E
Do - re - mi! Do - re - mi!

Solo

Do - re - mi - fa - so - la - ti

B REFRAIN

All

<u>Doe</u> — a deer, a female deer,
Low C

<u>Ray</u> — a drop of golden sun,
D

<u>Me</u> — a name I call myself,
E

<u>Far</u> — a long, long way to run.
F

<u>Sew</u> — a needle pulling thread,
G

<u>La</u> — a note to follow sew,
A

<u>Tea</u> — a drink with jam and bread
B

That will bring us back to <u>doe</u>!
    (Repeat refrain.)   **High C**

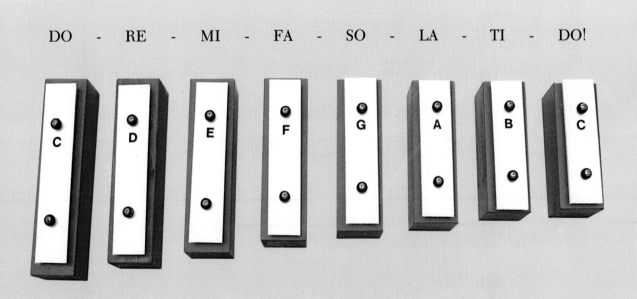

DO - RE - MI - FA - SO - LA - TI - DO!

STEP OR REPEAT

Find a pattern with repeated tones.

— — — — —

Find a pattern with stepping stones.

— — — — —

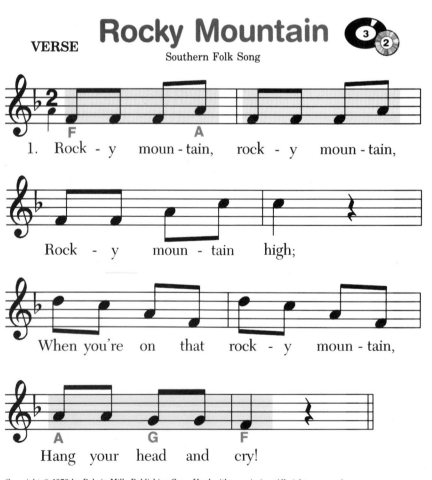

VERSE Rocky Mountain

Southern Folk Song

1. Rock - y moun - tain, rock - y moun - tain,

Rock - y moun - tain high;

When you're on that rock - y moun - tain,

Hang your head and cry!

REFRAIN

Do, do, do, do,

Do re - mem - ber me;

Do, do, do, do,

A G F

Do re - mem - ber me.

2. Sunny valley, sunny valley,
   Sunny valley low;
   When you're in that
   sunny valley,
   Sing it soft and slow.
   Refrain

3. Stormy ocean, stormy ocean,
   Stormy ocean wide;
   When you're on that deep
   blue sea,
   There's no place you can hide.
   Refrain

Play this bell part as an introduction.

Play it over and over with the song.

Do the bell tones repeat? Step? Leap?

High C

Low C

F

TONES THAT LEAP

Look at the yellow color box.

Some tones repeat and some tones leap.

— — —

            — — — —

     — — —   —

There Was a Little Woman

Folk Song from England

There was a lit - tle wom - an, As I've heard tell,

Fol, lol, did - dle, did - dle, dol;

She — went to mar - ket, Some eggs for to sell,

Fol, lol, did - dle, did - dle, dol;

High C   Low C

She went to mar - ket all on a mar - ket day,

And she fell a-sleep up-on the King's High-way;

Fol de rol de lol lol, lol lol lol,

Fol, lol, did-dle, did-dle, dol.

The Marketplace *John Sell Cotman*

PATTERNS OF MELODY

Find the steps, leaps, and repeated tones in this song.

Chumbara

French-Canadian Folk Song

1. Chum - ba - ra, _____ chum - ba - ra,

Chum - ba - ra, _____ chum - ba - ra,

Chum - ba - ra, _____ chum - ba - ra,

Chum, chum, chum, chum, chum, chum, chum, chum,

Chum - ba - ra, _____ chum - ba - ra,

Chum - ba - ra, _____ chum - ba - ra,

Chum - ba - ra, _____ chum - ba - ra, chum, chum!

2. Fy-do-lee   3. Chow-ber-ski

SING AND MOVE!

Some phrases in this song say "Dum-a-la-lum."
Find the "dum-a-la-lum" patterns
with this shape. ‒ ‒ ‒ ‒

Shake Hands, Mary

African-American Children's Song

1. Shake hands, Mar - y, Dum - a - la - lum. _

Shake hands, Mar - y, Dum - a - la - lum. _

REFRAIN

Lum, lum, lum, lum, Dum - a - la - lum. _

Lum, lum, lum, lum, Dum - a - la - lum. _

2. Strut, Mary,
   Dum-a-la-lum.
   Strut, Mary,
   Dum-a-la-lum. *Refrain*

3. Dance, Mary,
   Dum-a-la-lum.
   Dance, Mary,
   Dum-a-la-lum. *Refrain*

From PLAY SONGS OF THE DEEP SOUTH by Altona Trent-Johns. Copyright by
Association for the Study of Afro-American Life and History, Inc. Used by permission.

ONE VOICE, MANY VOICES

Listen to the recording.
Is the whole song sung by one voice?

Is it all sung by a group of voices?

Michael, Row the Boat Ashore

Black-American Work Song

Solo

1. Mich - ael,   row   the boat a - shore,

Chorus

Hal - le - lu - jah!

Solo

Mich - ael,   row   the boat a - shore,

Chorus

Hal - le - lu - jah!

2. Noah was a gentle man, . . .

3. Gabriel, blow the trumpet strong, . . .

4. Brother, help me turn the wheel, . . .

SHORT AND LONG SOUNDS

It is a sunny day.
Chickens, ducklings and geese come out to
play.

In the Barnyard

Music by Milton Kaye   Words by Dorothy Aldis

In __ the barn - yard chick - ens walk,

They jerk __ their heads __ and peck __ and talk

While yel - low duck - lings run a - round

Like but - ter - balls up - on the ground.

And some geese, tre - men - dous proud,

Point their nos - es at a cloud. _____

Show the long and short
movements of the animals.

Chickens: ♩ ♩ ♩ ♩   quarter notes

Ducklings: ♫ ♫ ♫ ♫   eighth notes

Geese: ♩ ♩   half notes

Move to the short sounds and longer
sounds in this music.

"Ballet of the Unhatched Chicks" from
Pictures at an Exhibition . . . . . Mussorgsky

It's Time to Dance!

Long ago there was no TV or radio.
People made their own entertainment.
They sang, danced, and played instruments.

Clear the Kitchen

As Sung in Pennsylvania by Emma Katurah Grenoble

Down in Vir - gin - ia one af - ter - noon,

We swept the floor with a brand new broom;

And then we all would form a ring,

And this is the song that we would sing: ___

REFRAIN

"Clear the kitch - en, young folks, old folks,

Clear the kitch - en, young folks, old folks.

Old Vir - gin - ia nev - er tires!"

Play patterns of long and short sounds.

Dancing feet: 4 ♩ ♫ ♫ ♫ ♫ :|| Repeat over and over.

Clear the kitch - en, clear the kitch - en!

Steady beat: 4 ♩ ♩ ♩ ♩ :|| Repeat over and over.

Young folks, old folks

Broom: 4 ♩ ♩ :|| Repeat over and over.

Swish, swish
Swish, swish

SOUND AND SILENCE

Where do you find this pattern? ♩ 𝄽 ♪ 𝄽

Mister Sun

Traditional

Oh, Mis - ter Sun, Sun, Mis - ter Gold-en Sun,

Please shine down on me.

Oh, Mis - ter Sun, Sun, Mis - ter Gold-en Sun,

Hid - ing be - hind a tree.

These lit - tle chil - dren are _____ ask - ing you

To please come out so we can play with you.

Oh, Mis-ter Sun, Sun, Mis-ter Gold-en Sun,

Please shine down on me. _____

This Happy Day

Every morning when the sun
Comes smiling up on everyone,
It's lots of fun
To say good morning to the sun.
  Good morning, Sun!

Every evening after play
When the sunshine goes away,
It's nice to say,
Thank you for this happy day,
  This happy day!

Harry Behn

Patterns in Names

Find the patterns for the
names in this song—

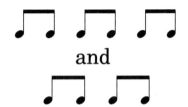

and

Polly Wolly Doodle

American Folk Song

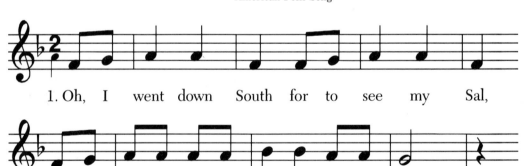

1. Oh, I went down South for to see my Sal,

Sing-ing Pol - ly Wol - ly Doo-dle all the day;

My __ Sal, she is a __ spunk - y gal,

Sing-ing Pol - ly Wol - ly Doo-dle all the day.

REFRAIN

Fare thee well, _____ fare thee well, _____

Fare thee well, my fair - y fay, _____

For I'm goin' to Lou' - si - an - a,

For to see my Su - sy - an - na,

Sing - ing Pol - ly Wol - ly Doo - dle all the day. _____

2. Oh, my Sal, she is a maiden fair,
   Singing Polly Wolly Doodle all the day;
   With curly eyes and laughing hair,
   Singing Polly Wolly Doodle all the day.
   Refrain

3. Behind the barn, down on my knees, . . .
   I thought I heard a chicken sneeze, . . .

4. He sneezed so hard with the whooping cough, . . .
   He sneezed his head and tail right off, . . .

THE MAN IN THE MOON

There was a man lived in the moon.
Find the pattern of his name.

Aiken Drum

Folk Song from the British Isles

1. There _ was a man lived in the moon,

Lived in the moon, lived in the moon,

There _ was a man lived in the moon,

And his name was Ai - ken Drum.

2. And his hat was made of good cream cheese, . . .
And his name was Aiken Drum.

3. And his coat was made of good roast beef, . . .

4. And his buttons were made of raisins, . . .

5. And he played upon a ladle, . . .

Play the sound of Aiken Drum's name—

Ai - ken Drum

EVEN OR UNEVEN?

Listen for the name *Lazy John* in this song.
Clap the rhythm pattern when you hear it.

La - zy   John

Lazy John

Words and Music by Alan Lomax and Jean Ritchie

1. La - zy John,   La - zy John,   Tell me where you've been.

Just got back from La - zy Town,

I'm go - in' back a - gain.

REFRAIN

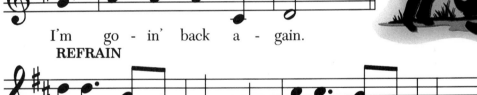

O - ho, ba - by, o - ho,   O - ho, ba - by, o - ho;

O - ho, ba - by, o - ho, I'm go - in' back a - gain.

2. Lazy John, Lazy John,
Tell me what you do.
Sit beside a hollow tree
And dream the whole day through.
Oho, baby, oho, *(3 times)*
And dream the whole day through.

Polka

Follow the chart below as you listen.
The numbers you hear will help you.

 "Polka" from *The Golden Age* . . .
. . . . Shostakovich

1. Introduction 2.  3.

4.

5.  6. 7.

8.  9.

10.  11.

12. Ending

This instrument
is a trombone.

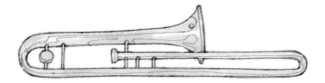

Did you hear its sliding sounds in "Polka"?
The trombone acts like a clown in this music.
It interrupts the other instruments.

Try to hear which other instruments the
trombone interrupts at number 5.

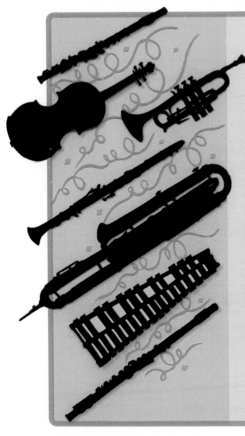

About the Music

"Polka" comes from a ballet called
The Golden Age. It was written by
Dmitri Shostakovich (dih MEE tree
SHAH stuh KOH vihtch). "Polka" is
an example of a musical joke. The
piece is full of short, happy-
sounding melodies. What a good
time Shostakovich must have had
writing it. And what fun
musicians have playing it!

A VISITOR

Listen for the things that the Butzemann
does in this song.

The Butzemann

Folk Melody from Germany   Words by Trudi Eichenlaub

There is a lit - tle But - ze - mann

Who danc - es round our house at night,

There is a lit - tle But - ze - mann

Who danc - es round our house.

He shakes like this and shakes like that,

Then flings his sack be - hind his back,

There is a lit - tle But - ze - mann

Who danc - es round our house.

SAY A PHRASE, SING A PHRASE

Who Has Seen the Wind?

Who has seen the wind?
  Neither I nor you:
But when the leaves hang trembling
  The wind is passing thro'.

Who has seen the wind?
  Neither you nor I:
But when the trees bow down their heads
  The wind is passing by.

Christina Rossetti

Who Has Seen the Wind?

Melody from *Zion's Harp*   Words by Christina Rossetti

1. Who has seen the wind? _____

Nei - ther I nor __ you!

But when the leaves hang trem - bling

The wind is pass - ing through,

The wind is pass - ing — through.

2. Who has seen the wind?
   Neither you nor I:
   But when the trees bow
     down their heads
   The wind is passing by,
   The wind is passing by.

Try moving to the phrases in this music.

"The Swan" from *Carnival of the Animals*............Saint-Saëns

A LULLABY

Find the phrases in this song.

At the Gate of Heav'n

Basque Folk Song

1. At the gate of heav'n they sell shoes for the an - gels,

Lit - tle bare-foot an - gels, oh, come now and buy them.

Sleep, my __ ba - by, Sleep, O my ba - by,

Sleep, __ O my ba - by, a - rru, a - rru.

2. God will send his blessing to
   all babes a-sleeping,
   God will help the mothers as
   watch they are keeping.
   Sleep, my baby,
   Sleep, O my baby,
   Sleep, O my baby, arru, arru.

How many long phrases did you sing?
How many short phrases did you sing?

FEELING LONG PHRASES

Face a different way for
each phrase.

Ninna-nanna

Folk Song from Italy   English Words by Ann Scibilia

Nin - na - nan - na, "Lul - la - by," sings the moth - er;

Nin - na - nan - na, "Lul - la - by, Lit - tle One." ___

Nin - na - nan - na, "Lul - la - by," sings the fa - ther;

Nin - na - nan - na, "Lul - la - by, day is done."

Ninna-nanna, còccolo della mamma; } 2 times
Ninna-nanna, còccolo del pappa.

Meow!

This song tells about a tomcat.
Listen for the story.

The Cat

Folk Melody from Brazil   Words by Verne Muñoz

1. The tom - cat has a ver - y nois - y song,

And he sings it for us all night long.

He al - ways sings the same me - ow, meow, meow,

You'd think he'd get tired of that;

He al - ways sings the same me - ow, meow, meow,

(Spoken)

You'd think he'd get tired of that. Me-ow! Scat!

2. I opened up the door and chased the cat;
Tomcat ran, that was the end of that!
But soon I heard that old meow,
   meow, meow,
I knew that the cat was back.
Meow! Scat!

} *2 times*

Listen for the sound of two cats in this music.

"Love for Two Cats" from *L'Enfant et les sortilèges* .Ravel

A Song with Two Sections

Pat your legs during section A.
Clap your hands during section B.

Built My Lady a Fine Brick House

Folk Song from Texas

A

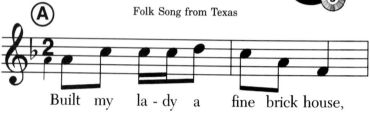

Built my la-dy a fine brick house,

Built it in a gar - den,

I put her in but she jumped out,

B REFRAIN

So fare ye well, — my dar - ling.

Oh, swing a la - dy ump - tum, swing a la - dy round,

Swing a la - dy ump - tum and prom - e - nade a - round.

An Action Song

Act out the words as you sing this song.

Scrapin' Up Sand

American Folk Song

A

1. Scrap-in' up the sand from the bot-tom of the sea,

Shi - loh! Shi - loh!

Scrap-in' up the sand from the bot-tom of the sea,

Shi-loh! Li - za Jane!

B REFRAIN

Oh, how I'll miss you! Oh, what a shame!

Oh, how I'll miss you! Bye, bye, Li - za Jane!

F♯ E D

2. Pickin' up the pears that have fallen from the tree, . . .

3. Pickin' out the weeds from the watermelon patch, . . .

Hello and Good-by

Move when you hear section A.
Stop and sing when you hear section B.

Come and Dance

American Folk Song   Words Adapted

1. Come a-long and dance with me, Come a-long and dance with me,

Come a-long and dance with me, Love-ly Su-sie Brown.

B REFRAIN

Fare thee well, my charm-ing girl, Fare thee well, I'm gone;

Fare thee well, my charm-ing girl, With gold-en slip-pers on.

2. Round the circle we will go,
   Round the circle we will go,
   Round the circle we will go,
   Lovely Susie Brown. *Refrain*

From *The American Songbag*, Carl Sandburg—compiler; Harcourt Brace Jovanovich, Inc.—publisher

A TALL TALE

These drawings show the two sections in "Old Dan Tucker."

Do you think the sections will sound the same or different?
Why?

Old Dan Tucker

American Folk Song

1. Old Dan Tuck-er was a might-y man,

He washed his face in the fry-ing pan,

Combed his hair with a wag-on wheel,

Had a tooth-ache in his heel;

So get out the way, Old Dan Tuck - er;

Get out the way, Old Dan Tuck - er;

Get out the way, Old Dan Tuck - er,

You're too late to get your sup - per.

2. Old Dan Tucker came to town,
   Riding a billy goat, leading a hound;
   Hound dog barked, then billy goat jumped;
   Dan fell off and landed on a stump; *Refrain*

ALL ABOARD!

This song has two different sections, A and B.
Which pattern below shows the form of the song?

1.  **2.**

Get on Board
African-American Spiritual

(A) Get on board, lit - tle chil - dren,

Get on board, lit - tle chil - dren,

Get on board, lit - tle chil - dren,

There's room for man - y - a more.

[B] The gos - pel train's a - com - ing,

I hear it close at hand, _____

I hear the car-wheels rum-bling

And roll-ing through the land.

A

Get on board, lit-tle chil-dren,

Get on board, lit-tle chil-dren,

Get on board, lit-tle chil-dren,

There's room for man-y-a more.

MINUET IN G

A minuet is a stately dance in ABA form.

Move with a partner during section A.

Move by yourself during section B.

Minuet in G . . .
. . . . . Beethoven

About the Music

Minuet in G was written by Ludwig van Beethoven (LOOD vihg van BAY toh vehn). In his day the minuet was a popular dance at court.

Listen to the graceful sounds of Beethoven's music. Imagine the people dancing in their beautiful clothes. Try to keep that feeling when you dance to the music.

You will hear five pieces of music.
Listen to each piece and decide how the
music moves.

Is it all fast?

Is it all slow?

Choose your answer when the music stops.

1. Fast   Slow

2. Fast   Slow

3. Fast   Slow

4. Fast   Slow

5. Fast   Slow

TEST 3

Some of these instruments need strings in order to play.

On your worksheet, draw strings on the instruments that need them.

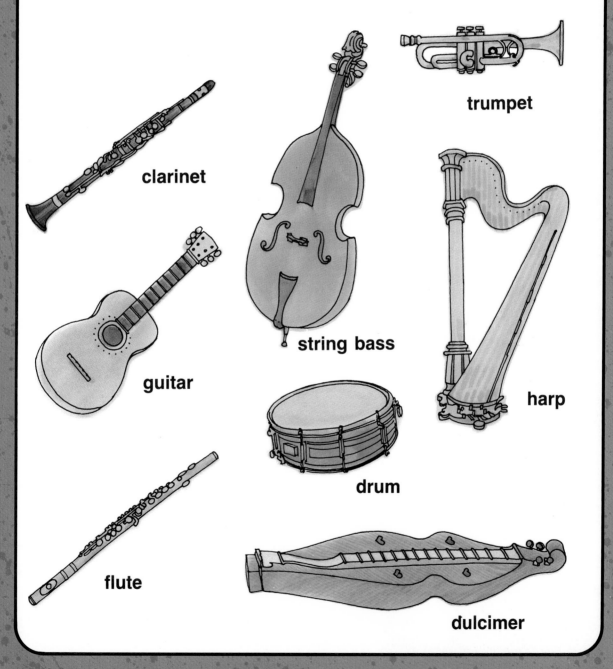

trumpet

clarinet

string bass

guitar

harp

drum

flute

dulcimer

TEST 4

A. Choose **S** if the notes move by *step*.
Choose **R** if the notes *repeat*.
Circle your answers on your worksheet.

1.   S   R

2.   S   R

3.   S   R

4.   S   R

5.   S   R

B. Choose **S** if the notes move by *step*.
Choose **L** if the notes *leap*.
Circle your answers on your worksheet.

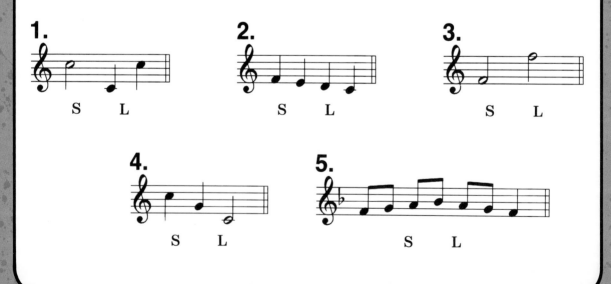

1.   S   L

2.   S   L

3.   S   L

4.   S   L

5.   S   L

You will hear five pieces of music.
Listen to each piece and decide how the tones move.
Do they mostly step?
Do they mostly leap?

Choose your answer when the music stops.

— — — — — — — — — — — — —

1.   Step   Leap

2.   Step   Leap

3.   Step   Leap

4.   Step   Leap

5.   Step   Leap

TEST 5

Each set of lines shows a rhythm pattern.
Can you show the patterns with notes?

Use *eighth notes*—♪♪—for the short
lines: __ __

Use a *quarter note*—♩—for each longer
line: ____

Use a *half note*—𝅗𝅥—for each very long
line: _____

Write your notes above the lines on
your worksheet.

1. _____ __ __ _____

2. ____ ____ _____

3. __ __ __ __ ___ ___

4. __ __ ___ __ __ ___

5. ____ __ __ __ ___

TEST 6

Each set of lines shows a rhythm pattern.
The notes beneath the lines also show
rhythm patterns.

In each example, choose the notes that
match the pattern of the lines.
Circle your answers on your worksheet.

1.

   a.   b.

2.

   a.   b.

3.

   a.   b.

4.

   a.   b.

5.

   a.   b.

You will hear five pieces of music.
Sometimes the music has mostly even
rhythm patterns.
Other times the music has mostly uneven
rhythm patterns.

Listen to each piece and decide what
you hear.

Choose your answer when the music stops.

1.   Even   Uneven

2.   Even   Uneven

3.   Even   Uneven

4.   Even   Uneven

5.   Even   Uneven

You will hear five pieces of music.
Sometimes the music ends with a
complete phrase:

Other times the music ends partway
through a phrase:

Listen to each piece and decide what
you hear.

Choose your answer when the music stops.

1.

2.

3.

4.

5.

TEST 7

A. One box in each row shows two different things, A and B.

Find it and circle it on your worksheet.

1.

2.

3.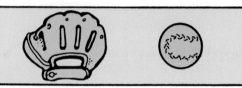

B. Make each set of boxes below show an AB design.

Does picture x or picture y belong in the empty box?
Circle that picture on your worksheet.

1. x.   y.

A   B

2. x.   y.

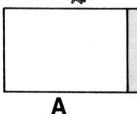

A   B

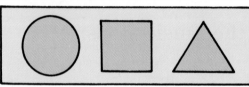

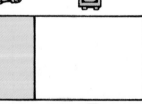

You will hear five pieces of music.
Some of the music has two sections—Ⓐ🄱.
The other music has three sections—
Ⓐ🄱Ⓐ.
Listen to each piece and decide what
you hear.
Choose your answer when the music stops.

1.

2.

3.

4.

5.

MAKING MUSIC

A PLAY-PARTY GAME

Listen to this song.
Can you hear which section repeats?

Shoo, Fly

American Game Song

Shoo, fly, don't both - er me, Shoo, fly, don't both - er me,

Shoo, fly, don't both - er me, For I be-long to some-bod - y.

I feel, I feel, I feel, I feel like a morn - ing star,

I feel, I feel, I feel, I feel, I feel like a morn - ing star. So,

Shoo, fly, don't both - er me, Shoo, fly, don't both - er me,

Shoo, fly, don't both - er me, For I be-long to some-bod - y.

AN ACTION SONG

You can perform motions
with this song.
The pictures will help you.

my

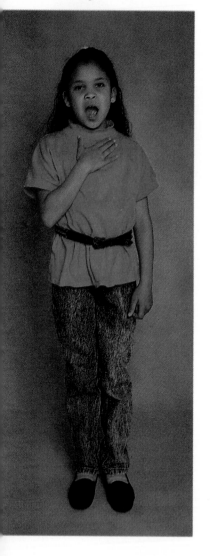

three

hat

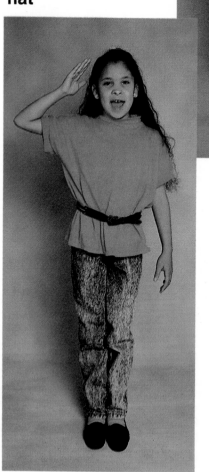

corners

My Hat

Folk Song from Germany

My hat it has three cor-ners; _____

Three cor-ners has my hat; _____

And had it not three cor-ners, _____

It would not be my hat. _____

CLAP AND CHANT

Listen for your name in this chant.
Can you say your part at the right time?

Cookie Jar

Playground Chant

All

Zoom, zoom, zoom, my heart goes ka - boom.

Now who stole the cook - ie from the cook - ie jar?

One Child*

(*Name*) stole the cook - ie from the cook - ie jar.

Child Named   **All**

Who, me? Yes, you!

Child Named   **All**

**Could - n't be! Then who?

FROM THE OLD WEST

Long ago, cowhands drove cattle along a trail from Texas to Kansas.

Think how the cowhands felt as they "pressed along" to Kansas.

The Big Corral

American Cowboy Song

The hus - ky brute from the cat - tle chute,

Press a - long to the big cor - ral!

He should be brand - ed on the snoot,

Press a - long to the big cor - ral!

B REFRAIN

Press a - long, cow - boy,

Press a - long with a cow - boy yell, Ya - hoo!

Press a - long, cow - boy,

Press a - long to the big cor - ral!

Play this bell part during section A.

Bells

F C D C   G C D C

F C D C

Play this pattern on wood block in Section B.

Play 4 times.

HUSH! CHILD SLEEPING

How will you sing this song, loud or soft?
Why?

Lullaby, My Jamie

Folk Song from Latvia   Words by Rose Stanfield

1. Lul - la - by, my Ja - mie,

Soft - ly sleep, my child,

Sis - ter gent - ly rocks you,

Light her hands and mild.

Reproduced by permission of Novello and Company Limited

2. Snow-white lambs for Jamie,
   All kinds for your own,
   Curly, bobtailed, longtailed,
   When a man you're grown.

Play the autoharp with a friend
as others sing.

The chord names in the music
will help you.

Listen to this music.
Would this music make a good lullaby?

"Invocation of the Powerful Spirits"
from *Panambé* . . . . Ginastera

WHERE IS THE FLOWER?

The Flower *(El florón)*

Singing Game from Puerto Rico   English Words by Verne Muñoz

Pass the flow - er round and a - round.

Will it be found? Will it be found?

Pass the flow - er round and a - round.

Will it be found? Will it be found? ___

Where is it? Where is it? Where can the flow - er be? ___

Where is it? Where is it? Where can the flow - er be? ___

El florón pasó por aquí, }
Yo no lo vi, Yo no lo vi. }   *2 times*

¿Que pase, que pase, }
Que pase el florón? }   *2 times*

144   **Songs to Sing with Instruments**

A FOLK DANCE

Ach ja!

Folk Song from Germany

Ⓐ

When my fa-ther and my moth-er make a vis-it to the fair,

Ach ja! Ach ja!

Though they have-n't an-y mon-ey, they're as rich as an-y there,

Ach ja! Ach ja!

Ⓑ REFRAIN

Tra la la, tra la la, tra la la la la la la la,

Tra la la, tra la la, tra la la la la la la la.

Ach ja! Ach ja!

SAYING GOODBYE

You can play the autoharp with this song.

Which chords will you play?

Go Well and Safely

Zulu Parting Song   English Words by Olcutt Sanders

Go   well ___   and   safe - ly,

Go   well ___   and   safe - ly,

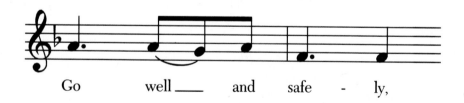

Go   well ___   and   safe - ly,

The   Lord   be   ev - er   with   you. _____

Ha-mba-ni ka-hle,
Ha-mba-ni ka-hle,
Ha-mba-ni ka-hle,
I nko-ni ma-yi-be na-ni.

146   **Songs to Sing with Instruments**

A TOE-TAPPING SONG

Sing and dance to "Jubilee!"

Jubilee!

Singing Game from Kentucky

A 1. All out on the old rail-road, All out on the sea;

All out on the old rail-road, Far as eye can see.

B REFRAIN

Swing an' turn, Ju - bi-lee! Live an' learn, Ju - bi-lee!

2. Hardest work I've ever done,
   Workin' on the farm;
   Easiest work I've ever done,
   Swingin' my true love's arm! *Refrain*

3. If I had me a needle and thread,
   Fine as I could sew,
   Sew my true love to my side,
   And down this creek I'd go. *Refrain*

4. If I had no horse to ride,
   I'd be found a-crawlin',
   Up and down this rocky road,
   Looking for my darlin'. *Refrain*

5. All out on the old railroad,
   All out on the sea;
   All out on the old railroad,
   Far as eye can see. *Refrain*

RONDE AND SALTARELLO

French School: *Ball at the Court of the Valois*, 16th Century. Bulloz, Paris.

This music is dance music.

Listen to the recording. Do you think
the dance was like the ones we do today?

Ronde .... Susato

Now listen to the same music played a different way.

Saltarello. . . . . Susato

About the Music

Ronde and *Saltarello* are dance pieces written in the 1500s by Tielman Susato (TEEL mahn soo ZAH toh). Susato wanted them played on any instruments that the people had. You have heard the dances played on brass instruments. How do you think they would sound on flutes? Or on violins? Or on guitar? *Ronde* and *Saltarello* have the same melody, but they use it in different ways.

DANCE A SONG

Listen for two different sections in this song. Which is repeated—A or B?

Run, Children, Run

African-American Folk Song   Words Adapted

Ⓐ
Run, chil-dren, run, it's time to hur-ry home now;

Run, chil-dren, run, the day is done.

Ⓑ
1. One child ran and one child flew,

And one child lost a Sun-day shoe.

Ⓐ
Run, chil-dren, run, it's time to hur-ry home now;

Run, chil-dren, run, the day is done.

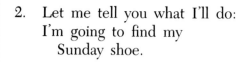

2. Let me tell you what I'll do:
   I'm going to find my
   Sunday shoe.

3. Let me tell you where I'll be:
   I'm going to look
   behind that tree.

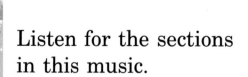

Listen for the sections
in this music.

"Run, Run" from *Memories of Childhood* . . . . Pinto

A Song to Sign

Sign language helps us speak to people who cannot hear.
Look at the pictures on page 155.
They show the signs for the words in this song.

My Father's House

Traditional American Song

1.–3. Won't you come with me to my fa-ther's house,

To my fa-ther's house, to my fa-ther's house?

Oh, won't you come with me to my fa-ther's house,

1. There is peace, peace, peace.

2. . . . There is joy, joy, joy.

3. . . . There is love, love, love.

Try to "sign" the song as you sing.

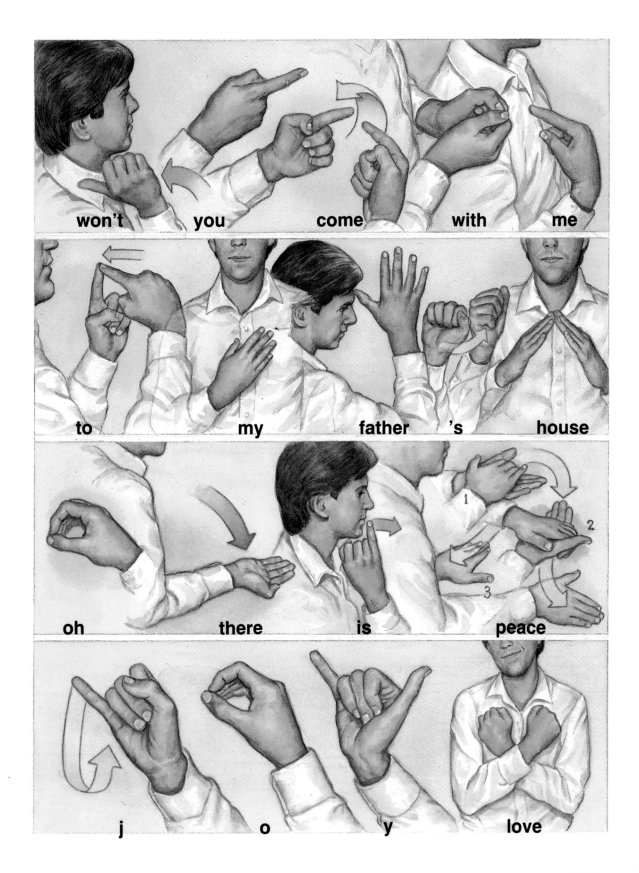

won't you come with me

to my father 's house

oh there is peace

j o y love

A QUIET TIME

Native American children take part in
the songs and dances of their nation.
At an early age they learn how to
beat a drum.
They also learn to shake rattles.

Sunset

Native American Song

Now the moon ——— is in the sky,

To the sun ——— we say good - bye;

Fa - ther Sun sleeps in the West.

In the sky ——— we see the moon;

Shad - ows creep, — the night comes soon;

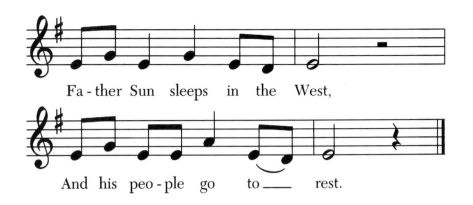

Fa - ther Sun sleeps in the West,

And his peo - ple go to ___ rest.

Play the steady beat on a tom-tom.

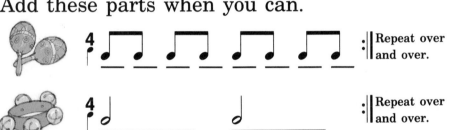

Repeat over and over.

Add these parts when you can.

Repeat over and over.

Repeat over and over.

AN ADD-ON SONG

You can create sound effects for this song.
Choose sounds that you like.

Goat Song

Folk Song from Italy   English Words by Leo Israel
Collected and Adapted by Rudolph Goehr

1. Oh, the   goat came skip-ping, From the   pas - ture trip-ping,

And he ate my shoe; Oh, ___ he nib-bled at my shoe!

Then he gob - bled up my shoe!

What to   do with just one   shoe! _____

2. Then the wolf came howling,
   When the goat came skipping,
   From the pasture tripping,
   And he ate my shoe;
   Oh, he nibbled at my shoe!
   Then he gobbled up my shoe!
   What to do with just one shoe!

3. Then the dog came barking,
   When the wolf came howling,
   When the goat came skipping . . .

4. Then the stick came beating,
   When the dog came barking,
   When the wolf came howling,
   When the goat came skipping . . .

5. Then a fire was burning,
   When the stick came beating,
   When the dog came barking,
   When the wolf came howling,
   When the goat came skipping . . .

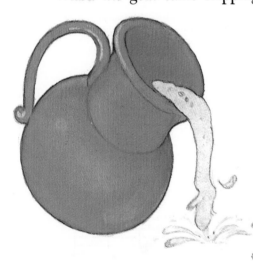

6. With the water pouring,
   When a fire was burning,
   When the stick came beating,
   When the dog was barking,
   When the wolf came howling,
   When the goat came skipping . . .

7. And I lay there sleeping,
   With the water pouring,
   When a fire was burning,
   When the stick came beating,
   When the dog came barking,
   When the wolf came howling,
   When the goat came skipping . . .

FINDING A PATTERN

Look for this short-short-long pattern in the song:

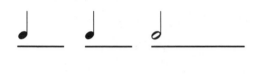

How many times do you see it?

Old John Braddelum

Folk Melody from England   Words Adapted

1. Num - ber one, Num - ber one,

Now my song has just be - gun.

REFRAIN

With a rum - tum tad - de - lum, Old John Brad - de - lum,

Hey, what hap - py folk are we!

2. Number two, Number two,
   You're with me and I'm with you.
   Refrain

3. Number three, Number three,
   This is easy as can be.
   Refrain

4. Number four, Number four,
   Just keep singing—we want more!
   Refrain

5. Number five, Number five,
   It's so great to be alive!
   Refrain

Listen for the tambourine in this music.
Which set of lines below shows the pattern
it plays?

1. __ __ ___   2. ___ __ __

Staines Morris Dance (excerpt) ....
.... **Anonymous**

SING AND SPEAK

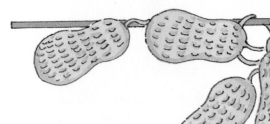

Peanut Butter

Camp Song

REFRAIN

Pea-nut, _ pea-nut but-ter, _ jel-ly!

VERSE

1. First you dig the pea-nuts, and you dig 'em, you dig 'em.

You dig 'em, dig 'em, dig 'em, then you crush 'em, you crush 'em.

You crush 'em, crush 'em, crush 'em, then you spread 'em, you spread 'em.

You spread 'em, spread 'em, spread 'em. *Refrain*

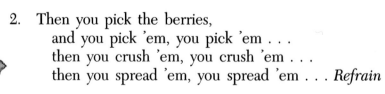

2. Then you pick the berries,
   and you pick 'em, you pick 'em . . .
   then you crush 'em, you crush 'em . . .
   then you spread 'em, you spread 'em . . . *Refrain*

3. Then you bite the sandwich,
   and you bite it, you bite it . . .
   and you munch it, you munch it, . . .
   then you swallow, you swallow . . . *Refrain*

RHYTHM PATTERNS TO PLAY

How many rhythm patterns can you find in this song.

How Good and Joyous

Hebrew Folk Song

How good and joy - ous it is _____

For broth-ers to dwell to - geth - er.

Good and joy - ous

For broth - ers to dwell to - geth - er.

Hi-neh mah tov u-ma na-im,
She-vet a-chim gam ya-chad. } *2 times*
Hi-neh mah tov,
She-vet a-chim gam ya-chad. } *2 times*

Play these patterns with the song.

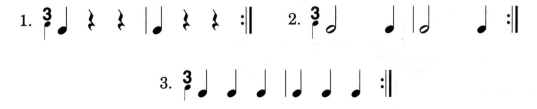

A MUSICAL SCENE

What sounds does the song tell about?
Listen for them on the recording.

Temple Bell

Melody from China   Words from a Chinese Poem   Adapted by Burton Kurth

1. Moun-tains hid in a mist-y cloud;

Bam-boos lin-ing the dust-y road.

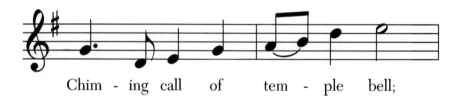

Chim-ing call of tem-ple bell;

Night is fall-ing on field and dell.

2.   Homeward come the weary feet
      Trudging down the village street,
      Welcomed by the sound of flute.
      Soon, oh, soon will all sounds be mute.

Now listen to this music from China.
It suggests the rising and the setting of
the moon.

High Moon . . . . Chinese

THE SNOW IS DANCING

Have you ever watched the snow fall?
Sometimes it changes as it falls?

Sometimes the snow swirls.

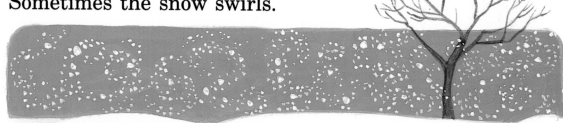

Sometimes it drops like a heavy curtain.

Sometimes the flakes seem to dance.

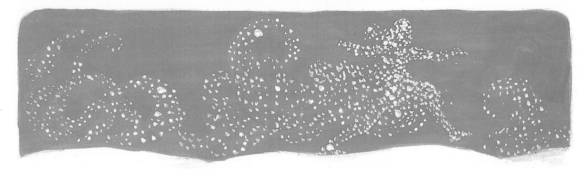

Try to picture the dancing snow in this music.

 "The Snow Is Dancing" from *Children's Corner Suite* . . . . Debussy

These lines show the shape of three melodies.
Can you hear the melodies in the music?

1.

2.

3.

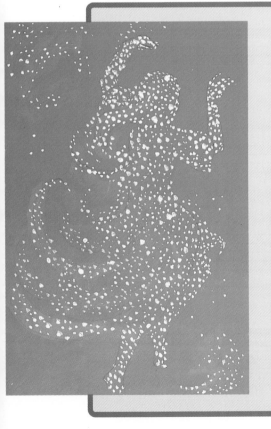

About the Music

Can you imagine a piece of music being a present? That's what "The Snow Is Dancing" was. This music is part of a larger work called *Children's Corner Suite*. Claude Debussy (klohd duh byew see) wrote *Children's Corner Suite* as a present for his daughter. There are five other pieces in *Children's Corner Suite*. One of them is a lullaby for an elephant. Another one is a lively dance called "Golliwog's Cakewalk."

A STORY SONG

Market Song

Folk Song from Italy   English Words by Leo Israel
Collected and Adapted by Rudolph Goehr

All
1. One day my moth-er went to the mar - ket

And she bought a hand-some roost - er.

Solo   *Chorus*
A roost - er?   A roost - er!

All
But when my moth-er start-ed to cook him,

He did ev' - ry - thing he use - ta.

Solo   *Chorus*
He use - ta?   He use - ta!

All
Oh, he said, "Cock - a - doo - dle - doo,

How I love you, how I love you."

Oh, he said, "Cock - a - doo - dle - doo,"

And a - way he flew, and a - way he flew.

2. . . . and she bought a little pig . . .
But when my mother started to cook him,
He got up and danced a jig . . .
Oh, he said, "Oink, oink, oink,
Though I'd like to stay, though I'd like to stay."
Oh, he said, "Oink, oink, oink,"
And he ran away, and he ran away.

3. . . . and she bought a pretty lamb . . .
But when my mother started to cook him,
He said, "Who do you think I am?" . . .
Oh, he said, "Baa, baa, baa,
I'm silly, it's true, I'm silly, it's true."
Oh, he said, "Baa, baa, baa,
Not as silly as you, not as silly as you."

4. . . . and she bought a lovely hen . . .
But when my mother started to cook her,
She began to cluck again . . .
Oh, she said, "Cluck, cluck, cluck, cluck, cluck."
But she forgot, but she forgot,
Oh, she said, "Cluck, cluck, cluck, cluck, cluck,"
And fell into the pot, and fell into the pot.

Hoot and Holler!

Listen for the sound effects in this song.
Try to perform them with the recording.

She'll Be Comin' Round the Mountain

Southern Mountain Song

1. She'll be com-in' round the moun-tain when she comes, *(Toot, toot!)*

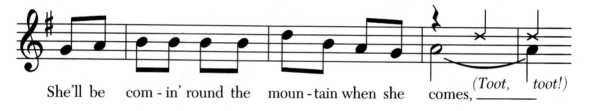

She'll be com-in' round the moun-tain when she comes, *(Toot, toot!)*

She'll be com-in' round the moun-tain,

She'll be com-in' round the moun-tain,

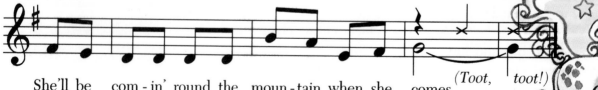

She'll be com-in' round the moun-tain when she comes. *(Toot, toot!)*

2. She'll be drivin' six white horses when she comes,
   (*Whoa, back!*)

3. Oh, we'll kill the old red rooster when she comes,
   (*Chop, chop!*)

4. Oh, we'll all have chicken and dumplin's when she comes,
   (*Yum, yum!*)

5. Oh, we'll all go out to meet her when she comes,
   (*Hi, there!*)

A SURPRISE

Have you ever had a surprise?

In this song a surprise comes from a root.
Can you discover what it is?

From a Lovely Root

1. From a love-ly root in the glen __

Came a fine and love-ly __ tree.

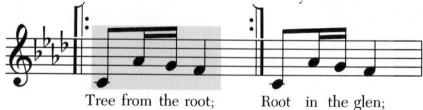

Tree from the root;   Root in the glen;

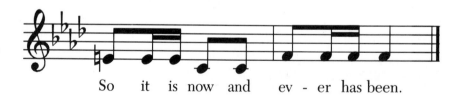

So it is now and ev-er has been.

2. On the tree that came from the root
   Grew a fine and lovely branch.
   Branch on the tree;
   Tree from the root;
   Root in the glen;
   So it is now and ever has been.

3. On the branch that grew on the tree
   Sat a fine and lovely nest.
   Nest on the branch . . .

4. In the nest that sat on the branch
   Sang a fine and lovely bird.
   Bird in the nest . . .

5. On the bird that sang in the nest
   Grew some fine and lovely feathers.
   Feathers on the bird . . .

6. From the lovely feathers on the bird
   Came a fine and lovely pillow.
   Pillow from the feathers . . .

WAKE UP!

Every morning starts a new day.

How does the person in this song
feel each morning?
Which words tell you so?

Every Mornin'

Words and Music by Avon Gillespie

Ev - e - ry morn - in' when I wake — up

I have a new song to sing, my chil - dren,

Ev - e - ry morn - in' when I wake — up

I have a new song to sing.

Play a bell part while others sing
"Every Mornin'."

Follow the notes in color boxes.
The letters under the notes tell which bells
to play.

Let's Have a Parade!

Can you hear these instruments on the recording?

Point to the picture that shows the instrument you hear.

trumpet

tuba

trombone

piccolo

The Very Best Band

Words and Music by Joe Hampson

We have a band, —— the ver-y best band ——

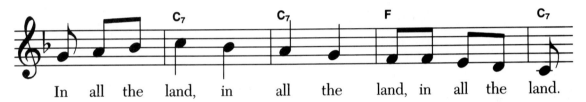

In all the land, in all the land, in all the land.

We have a band, —— the ver-y best band ——

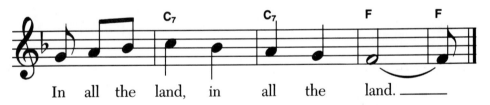

In all the land, in all the land. ——

This music is often played by parade bands.
Listen for the sound of the piccolo.
Does the piccolo play the same melody as
the other instruments?

The Stars and Stripes Forever
(excerpt)...............Sousa

A Theme Musical
by
Carmino Ravosa

HANDLE WITH CARE

BEST FRIENDS

Welcome to *Friends,* a play about friendship.

Best Friends

Music by Carmino Ravosa   Words by Margaret Jones

REFRAIN

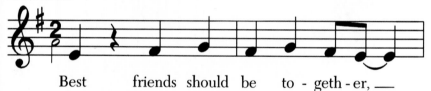

Best friends should be to - geth - er, —

That's how it ought to be; —

So let's pre - tend I'm part of — you,

(cue size notes last time)

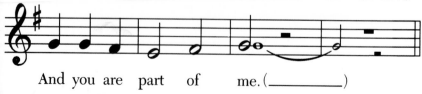

And you are part of me. (_____)

VERSES

1. If I were a little dog,
   I'd be your bow-wow;
   If I were a little cat,
   I'd be your meow.
   If I were a little owl,
   I could be your hoot;
   If I were a little train,
   I could be your toot. *Refrain*

2. If I were a lion,
   I could be your cage;
   If I were a little book,
   I could be your page.
   If I were a circus,
   I could be your clown;
   If I were a royal king,
   I could be your crown. *Refrain*

3. If I were a kangaroo,
   I could be your pouch;
   If I were a little scratch,
   I could be your ouch!
   If I were an apple,
   I could be your core;
   But if I were nothing,
   I'd like you even more. *Refrain*

MAKE A FRIEND

This is the boy's first day at school.
The teacher told him to make a friend.
He did—in a very unusual way.

Make a Friend

Words and Music by Carmino Ravosa

Solo — Make a friend to - day. *Chorus* — Make a friend to - day.

Solo — Make a friend to - day. *Chorus* — Make a friend to - day.

Solo — Then have fun and play, *Chorus* — Then have fun and play

Solo — With a friend to - day. *Chorus* — With a friend to - day.

Solo — Make a friend for you. *Chorus* — Make a friend for you.

Solo — Make a friend for you. *Chorus* — Make a friend for you.

YOU AND ME

Friends are important.
You and me—
we're the best of company!

You and Me

Words and Music by Carmino Ravosa

Pair 1

You and __ me,   You and __ me,

We're the best of com - pa - ny.

Pair 2

You and __ me,   You and __ me,

We are just like fam - i - ly.

Pair 1

When you cry, so do I.

Pair 2

When you're blue, I am, too.

Pairs 1 and 2

You and _ me, You and _ me,

We'll go down in his - to - ry.

You and _ me, You and _ me,

We're the best of friends, you see.

I Like You Like You Are

Please come out of that box!
You're <u>not</u> a monster!
I like you like you are!

HANDLE
WITH
CARE

I Like You Like You Are

Words and Music by Carmino Ravosa

I like you like you are, I like you like you are;

Don't change a thing, I like you like you are.

I like the things you do, I like the things you say;

I real - ly would-n't have you an - y oth - er way.

I like you like you are, I like you like you are;

Don't change a thing, I like you like you are.

THAT'S WHAT FRIENDS ARE FOR

Friends are honest with each other.
That's what friends are for!

That's What Friends Are For

Words and Music by Carmino Ravosa

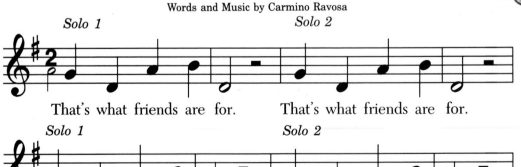

That's what friends are for.   That's what friends are for.

That's what friends are for.   That's what friends are for.

Solo 1

You don't have to thank me, 'Cause that's what friends are for.

(Solo 1 on Verse 1)
(Solo 2 on Verse 2)

1. Who else would play with you and not com - plain,
2. Who else would tell you that you are o - kay,

E-ven though ___ you real-ly are a pain?
E-ven though ___ you al-ways want your way?

Solos 1, 2   *Chorus*

That's what friends are for.   That's what friends are for.

Solos 1, 2   *Chorus*

That's what friends are for.   That's what friends are for.

Slower
All

You don't have to thank me,

'Cause that's what friends are for. _____

LET'S GO OUT AND PLAY

When you have friends, enjoy them.
Go out and play with them.

Let's Go Out and Play

Music by Carmino Ravosa   Words by Margaret Jones

Introduction, Solo 1
Listen to the birdies singing in the trees,
Listen to the flowers whisper to the bees;
Mister Sun is touching ev'rything he sees,
It's a lovely day,
Let's go out and play!

Solo 2
All the frogs are laughing, leaping as they go,
And the little ducks are swimming in a row;
Hear the chickens clucking and the rooster's crow,
It's a lovely day,
Let's go out and play!

Solo 3

We'll ride on the mer-ry-go-round, grab a ring;

Fol-low the lead-er, then hop on the swing.

You can chase me and then I will chase you;

We'll have fun like the chick-ens and frog-gies all do.

Solo 4
When it starts a-raining, then we'll stay inside,
Can't go on a seesaw or go down a slide.
Open all the windows and the doors up wide,

All { It's a lovely day,
Soloists { Let's go out and play!

© 1985 Carmino Ravosa and Margaret Jones

YOU CAN'T BUY FRIENDSHIP

Friendship is something
that you cannot buy.
Friendship is a gift.

You Can't Buy Friendship

Words and Music by Carmino Ravosa

You can't buy friend-ship, You can't buy love.

That's one thing I'm cer-tain of.

You've got to give be-fore you re-ceive;

You've got to trust, You've got to be-lieve.

© 1984 Carmino Ravosa

You can't buy friend-ship, You can't buy love.

It's a gift from up a-bove.

And if you're luck-y, And if you're true,

Then may-be love will come to you.

TEST 8

The people below are pretending to play instruments.
Can you name each instrument?
Choose your answers from the list.

Write your answers in the blanks on your worksheet.

autoharp   woodblock   bells

tambourine   piano   triangle

1. _____   2. _____   3. _____

4. _____   5. _____   6. _____

Write the name of each instrument under
its picture on your worksheet.

tuba   violin   guitar
flute   piccolo   xylophone
trombone   trumpet   piano

   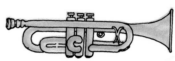   

1. _____ 2. _____ 3. _____

      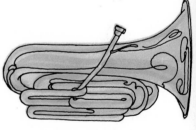

4. _____ 5. _____ 6. _____

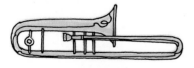      

7. _____ 8. _____ 9. _____

Jan 1 2 3 4 5 6	**Jul** 1 2 3 4 5 6
7 8 9 10 11 12 13 14 15	7 8 9 10 11 12 13 14 15
16 17 18 19 20 21 22 23 24	16 17 18 19 20 21 22 23 24
25 26 27 28 29 30 31	25 26 27 28 29 30 31
Feb 1 2 3 4 5 6	**Aug** 1 2 3 4 5 6
7 8 9 10 11 12 13 14 15	7 8 9 10 11 12 13 14 15
16 17 18 19 20 21 22 23 24	16 17 18 19 20 21 22 23 24
25 26 27 28	25 26 27 28 29 30 31
Mar 1 2 3 4 5 6	**Sep** 1 2 3 4 5 6
7 8 9 10 11 12 13 14 15	7 8 9 10 11 12 13 14 15
16 17 18 19 20 21 22 23 24	16 17 18 19 20 21 22 23 24
25 26 27 28 29 30 31	25 26 27 28 29 30
Apr 1 2 3 4 5 6	**Oct** 1 2 3 4 5 6
7 8 9 10 11 12 13 14 15	7 8 9 10 **31** 12 13 14 15
16 17 18 19 20 21 22 23 24	16 17 18 19 20 21 22 23 24
25 26 27 28 29 30	25 26 27 28 29 30 31
May 1 2 3 4 5 6	**Nov** 1 2 3 4 5 6
7 8 9 10 11 12 13 14 15	7 8 9 10 11 12 13 14 15
16 17 18 19 20 21 22 23 24	16 17 18 19 20 21 22 23 24
25 26 27 28 29 30	25 26 27 28 29 30
Jun 1 2 3 4 5 6	**Dec** 1 2 3 4 5 6
7 8 9 10 11 12 13 14 15	7 8 9 10 11 12 13 14 15
16 17 18 19 20 21 22 23 24	16 17 18 19 20 21 22 23 24
25 26 27 28 29 30	25 26 27 28 29 30 31

Boo!

On Halloween

Words and Music by Max T. Krone

1. Gob - lins, al - ley cats, witch - es on brooms,

Wind in the trees sing - ing scar - y tunes,

These are the things that are heard and seen,

In the dark of night, on Hal - low - een.

2. Rattling skeletons, ghosts in white,
   Moaning and groaning through the night,
   These are the things that are heard and seen,
   In the dark of night, on Halloween.

From "Discovering Music Together 2", copyright © Follett Publishing Co., 1967.
Reprinted by permission of Allyn and Bacon, Inc.

Listen to the scary sounds in this music.
Are they made by a voice or an instrument?

The Banshee. . . . . Cowell

SPOOKY SOUNDS

What things does this song tell you about the witch?

What sounds will you choose to describe her?

There Once Was a Witch

Traditional

1. There once was a witch, Be - lieve it if you can,

She tapped on the win-dows and she ran, ran, — ran.

She ran hel - ter - skel - ter with her toes in the air,

Corn - stalks fly - ing from the witch - 's hair!

2. "Swish," goes the broomstick.
"Meow," goes the cat.
"Plop," goes the hoptoad
 sitting on her hat.
"Whee!" chuckled I,
 "What fun! What fun!"
Halloween night when the
 witches run.

GUESS WHO!

The child in this song does not want to be recognized on Halloween.
What costumes does the child try out?

How Did You Know?

Words and Music by Linda Williams

1. Well, I took my-self to the cos-tume shelf

For a Hal - low - een dis - guise;

And I real - ly thought that an as - tro - naut

Was a ver - y good sur - prise.

But still you knew me right a - way,

As eas - y as could be;

Now how did you know, did you know, did you know,

How did you know it's me?

2. So I made a stop at a costume shop
   And I dressed up like a knight;
   And I looked so great in my armor plate,
   I was sure I'd done it right.
   But then I heard you say, "Hello,
   You're back again, I see!"
   Now how could you tell, could you tell,
   could you tell,
   How could you tell it's me?

3. Then I went right back to the laundry stack
   And I found a king-size sheet;
   Now I look just right, I'm a ghostly white
   From my head down to my feet.
   With just two very tiny holes,
   Enough for me to see;
   Now you'll never guess, never guess,
   never guess,
   You'll never guess it's me!

BEING THANKFUL

In November we set aside a day for giving thanks.

Thanksgiving

Folk Tune from Finland   English Words by Rosemary Jacques

1. For the sun that gives us light,

We are tru - ly thank - ful.

For the moon that shines at night,

We are tru - ly thank - ful.

For the twin-kling stars so __ bright,

We are tru - ly thank - ful.

2. For the corn and golden wheat,
   We are truly thankful.
   For the pears and apples sweet . . .
   For the good food that we eat . . .

3. For the joys of each new day . . .
   For each hour of work and play . . .
   For God's blessings, let us say,
   "We are truly thankful."

THANKSGIVING   *Doris Lee*

Doris Lee,
Thanksgiving, The Art Institute of Chicago, Mr. and Mrs. Frank G. Logan Purchase Prize, Chicago

A HOLIDAY VISIT

AMERICAN WINTER SCENES   *Currier and Ives*

Currier and Ives, American Winter Scenes, Museum of the City of New York, New York

Over the River and Through the Wood

Traditional   Words by Lydia Maria Child

1. O - ver the riv - er and through the wood,

To grand - fa - ther's house we go; _____

The horse knows the way to car - ry the sleigh

Thro' the white and drift - ed snow.____

O - ver the riv - er and through the wood,

Oh, how the wind does blow!____

It stings the toes and bites the nose

As o - ver the ground we go.

2. Over the river and through the wood,
   Trot fast, my dapple gray!
   Spring over the ground like a
      hunting hound,
   For this is Thanksgiving Day!

   Over the river and through the wood,
   Now grandmother's face I spy!
   Hurrah for the fun! Is the
      pudding done?
   Hurrah for the pumpkin pie!

A Musical Sleigh Ride . . . . . . L. Mozart

A Celebration

Candles are lighted for Chanukah.
How many are lighted on the
first night?   On the last night?

In the Window

Jewish Folk Melody   English Words by Judith K. Eisenstein

1. In the win - dow, where you can send your glow

From my Me - no - rah on new - ly fall - en snow,

I will set you one lit - tle can - dle

On this the first night of Cha - nu - kah.

2. In the window, where you can send your glow
   From my Menorah on newly fallen snow,
   I will set you two little candles
   On this the second night of Chanukah.

3. . . . three . . . third . . .	6. . . . six . . . sixth . . .
4. . . . four . . . fourth . . .	7. . . . seven . . . seventh . . .
5. . . . five . . . fifth . . .	8. . . . eight . . . eighth . . .

From THE GATEWAY TO JEWISH SONG by Judith Eisenstein. Reprinted by permission of the author.

SPIN THE DREYDL

Children sing songs and play games to celebrate Chanukah.

This song tells about the dreydl game.

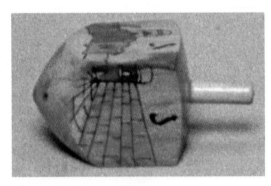

Joyous Chanukah

Hebrew Folk Song   English Words by Phyllis Resnick

Cha - nu - kah,   Cha - nu - kah,   hol - i - day so   fair,

Glow - ing light,   can - dles bright,   hap - pi - ness we   share.

Gai - ly dance,   gai - ly sing   while the drey - dl   whirls,

Round and round,   round and round,   see how fast it   twirls.

Here is a part to play on the tambourine.

Shake

Repeat 3 times.

A Story Song

Frosty, the Snowman

Words and Music by Steve Nelson and Jack Rollins

1. Fros - ty, the Snow - man, was a jol - ly, hap - py soul, ____

With a corn - cob pipe and a but - ton nose ____

And two eyes made out of coal.

Fros - ty, the Snow - man, is a fair - y tale, they say, ____

He was made of snow, but the chil - dren know ____

How he came to life one day.

There must have been some mag - ic in that old silk hat they found;

For when they placed it on his head,

He be-gan to dance a-round.

Oh, Fros-ty, the Snow-man, was a-live as he could be, ___

And the chil-dren say he could laugh and play ___

Just the same as you and me.

2. Frosty, the Snowman, knew the sun was hot that day,
So he said, "Let's run and we'll have some fun
Now before I melt away."
Down to the village, with a broomstick in his hand,
Running here and there all around the square,
Sayin', "Catch me if you can."
He led them down the streets of town right to
   the traffic cop,
And he only paused a moment
When he heard him holler "Stop!"
For Frosty, the Snowman, had to hurry on his way,
But he waved goodbye sayin', "Don't you cry,
I'll be back again some day."

TRIMMING THE TREE

Christmas! A time of green branches and bright lights!

O Christmas Tree

Folk Song from Germany   Words Adapted by Elsie Plant

O Christ - mas tree, O Christ - mas tree,

How ev - er green your branch - es.

1. You nev - er change the whole year round,

You bright - en up the snow - y ground.

O Christ - mas tree, O Christ - mas tree,

How ev - er green your branch - es!

2. We trim the tree at Christmastime,
And merry bells begin to chime.

Listen to this music.
Try to picture a party scene with a
beautiful Christmas tree.

"March" from *The Nutcracker* ......
.... Tchaikovsky

CAROLING, CAROLING

Carols from many different countries are heard at Christmastime.

This carol comes from Poland.

In a Manger

Carol from Poland   English Words by Rosemary Jacques

A

In a man - ger,   in a sta - ble,

Long a - go   on   Christ - mas day,

Lay a ti - ny   lit - tle ba - by

On a blan - ket   made of hay.

B

1. With his moth - er   watch - ing o'er him,

Ox and sheep knelt down be - fore him;

Al - le - lu - ia, he is born.

2. High above the heav'ns were
      ringing
   With the sound of angels'
      singing;
   Alleluia, he is born.

3. Shepherds brought their lambs
      to greet him,
   Wise Men journeyed far to
      meet him;
   Alleluia, he is born.

A CONVERSATION

Can you find another name for Saint Nicholas in this song?

Jolly Old Saint Nicholas

Traditional

1. Jol - ly old Saint Ni - cho - las, Lean your ear this way,

Don't you tell a sin - gle soul What I'm going to say;

Christ - mas Eve is com - ing soon, Now, you dear old man,

Whis - per what you'll bring to me, Tell me if you can.

2. When the clock is striking twelve,
   When I'm fast asleep,
   Down the chimney tall and round,
   With your pack you'll creep;
   All the stockings you will find
   Hanging in a row;
   Mine will be the shortest one,
   You'll be sure to know.

3. Johnny wants a pair of skates,
   Susie wants a toy,
   Nancy wants a story book,
   One to bring her joy;
   As for me, I'm not too sure,
   So I'll say "goodnight,"
   Choose for me, dear Santa Claus,
   What you think is right.

A GENTLE CAROL

Children in Norway sing this carol
at Christmas.

I Am So Glad on Christmas Eve

Carol from Norway   English Words by Sigrid Hansen

1. I am so glad ___ on Christ-mas Eve,

For then the child ___ was born; ___

Sweet an - gel voic - es filled the night,

And skies shone bright ___ as morn. ___

2. The little child of Bethlehem
   Came down from heaven above
   To bring to all upon the earth
   The message of his love.

FOUR SCENES

Each verse of this song describes a scene. Try to picture the scenes as you read the words.

Long, Long Ago

Traditional Carol

1. Winds through the   ol - ive trees

Soft - ly   did   blow

'Round lit - tle Beth - le - hem,

Long,   long   a - go.

2. Sheep on the hillside lay,
   Whiter than snow,
   Angels were watching them,
   Long, long ago.

3. Then from the happy sky,
   Angels bent low,
   Singing their songs of joy,
   Long, long ago.

4. Then from a manger bed,
   Cradled, we know,
   Christ came to Bethlehem,
   Long, long ago.

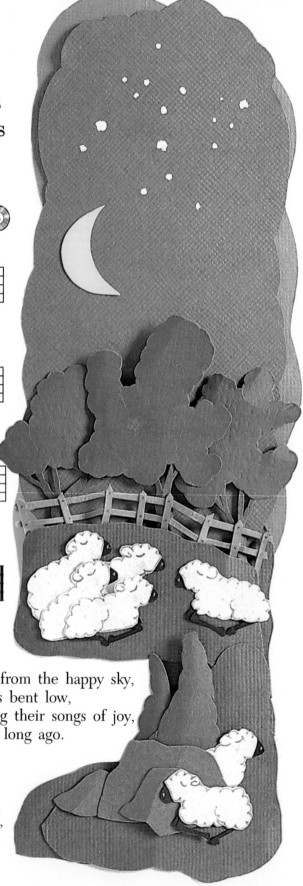

A Famous Carol

"Silent Night" was written because a church
organ broke down.
It is one of the world's best-loved carols.

Silent Night

Music by Franz Gruber   Words by Joseph Mohr

Si - lent night,   ho - ly night,

All   is   calm,   all   is   bright

Round yon Vir - gin   Moth - er and Child.

Ho - ly   In - fant so   ten - der and mild,

Sleep   in heav - en - ly   peace, ___

Sleep ___ in heav - en - ly   peace. ___

A SLEIGH RIDE

Have you ever been on a sleigh ride?
Can you imagine what it would be like?

Jingle Bells

Words and Music by James Pierpont

Dash-ing through the snow,   In a one-horse o - pen sleigh,

O'er the fields we   go,   Laugh - ing   all   the   way.

Bells   on   Bob - tail   ring,   Mak - ing   spir - its   bright;

What   fun   it   is   to   ride   and   sing

A   sleigh - ing   song   to - night!

REFRAIN

Jin - gle   bells,   jin - gle   bells,   Jin - gle   all   the   way!

Oh, what fun it is to ride

In a one-horse o-pen sleigh! __

Jin-gle bells, jin-gle bells, Jin-gle all the way!

Oh, what fun it is to ride

In a one-horse o-pen sleigh!

A CELEBRATION

Children in Spain sing this song
at Christmastime.

Zumba, Zumba

Folk Song from Spain   English Words by Margaret Marks

A REFRAIN

¡Zum - ba, zum - ba! Strike the cym - bal.

¡Zum - ba, zum - ba! Strike the gong.

¡Zum - ba, zum - ba! Beat the tim - bal

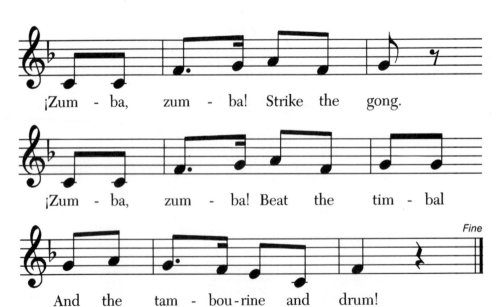

And the tam - bou - rine and drum!

B VERSE

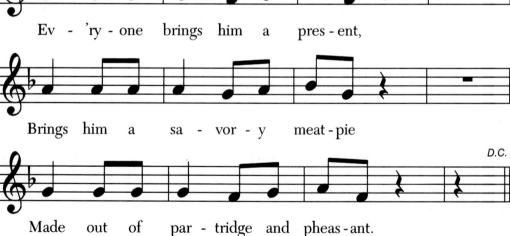

1. Born on this night is a ba-by.

Ev - 'ry - one brings him a pres-ent,

Brings him a sa - vor - y meat-pie

D.C.

Made out of par - tridge and pheas-ant.

2. What shall I take to the baby?
   What shall I say when I take it?
   I'll bring a gourd for a rattle,
   I'll ask his mother to shake it.

A MUSICAL VALENTINE

When is Valentine's Day?
Will you make valentines to send?

Somebody Loves Me

Words and Music by Gaynor Jones

Some-bod-y loves me, I won-der who?

Some-bod-y loves me, I won-der who?

Sent me this val-en-tine, All red and white;

Sent me this val-en-tine, Such a pret-ty sight.

Some-bod-y loves me, I won-der who?

Some-bod-y loves me, May-be you.

Reprinted and recorded by permission of Gaynor Jones Lowe

PLEASE BE MINE

Sunshine is very important to us.
It gives us warmth and light.

What does it mean to tell someone
"You are my sunshine"?

You Are My Sunshine

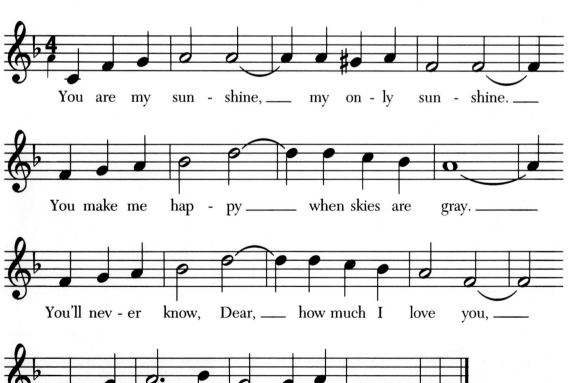

Words and Music by Jimmie Davis and Charles Mitchell

You are my sun - shine, ___ my on - ly sun - shine. ___

You make me hap - py ___ when skies are gray. ___

You'll nev - er know, Dear, ___ how much I love you, ___

Please don't take my sun - shine a - way. ___

OUR WONDERFUL HOME

We are proud of our country.
We sing songs that tell of its freedom.

America

Traditional   Words by Samuel Francis Smith

1. My coun - try! 'tis of thee, Sweet land of lib - er - ty,

Of thee I sing;

Land where my fa - thers died, Land of the Pil - grims' pride,

From ev - 'ry __ moun - tain - side

Let __ free - dom ring!

2. Our fathers' God, to Thee,
    Author of liberty,
    To Thee we sing;
    Long may our land be bright
    With Freedom's holy light;
    Protect us by Thy might,
    Great God, our King!

An Old Favorite

Yankee Doodle

Traditional   Words by Dr. Richard Shuckburgh

1. Fath'r and I went down to camp,

A - long with Cap - tain Good - in',

And there we saw the men and boys

As thick as hast - y pud - din'.

REFRAIN

Yan - kee Doo - dle, keep it up,   Yan - kee Doo - dle dan - dy,

Mind the mu - sic   and the step And with the girls be   hand - y.

2. And there was Captain Washington
   Upon a slappin' stallion,
   A-giving orders to his men;
   I guess there was a million. *Refrain*

THE FLAG

A flag is a symbol of a country.
Our flag is a symbol of America.

It stands for everything that Americans
hold dear.

There Are Many Flags

Traditional   Words by Mary H. Howliston

There are man - y flags in man - y lands,

There are flags of ev - 'ry hue;

But there is no flag, how - ev - er grand,

Like our own Red, White, _ and _ Blue.

REFRAIN

Then hur - rah for the flag, our coun - try's flag,

Its stripes and its white stars, too,

For there is no flag in an - y land

Like our own Red, White, _ and _ Blue.

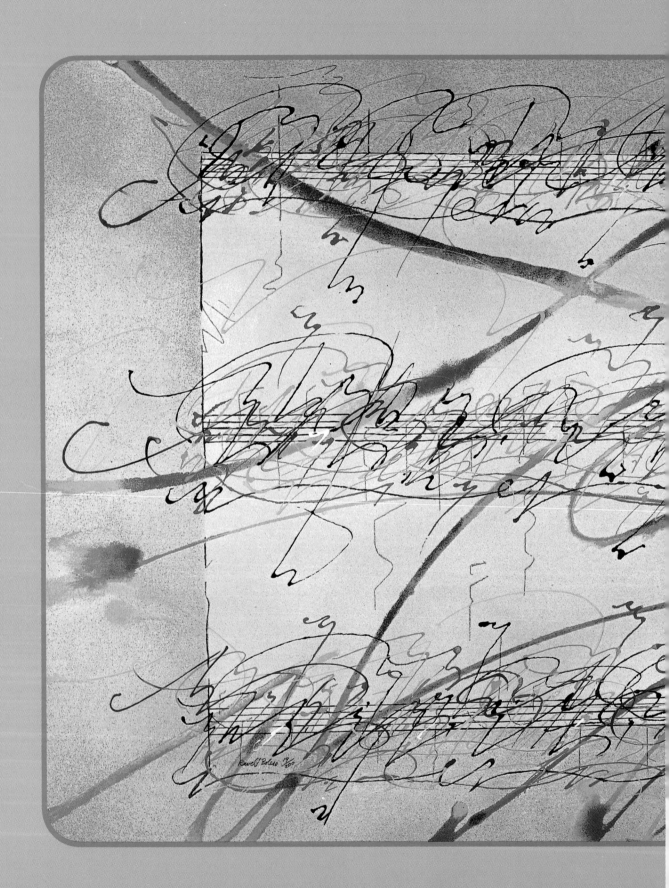

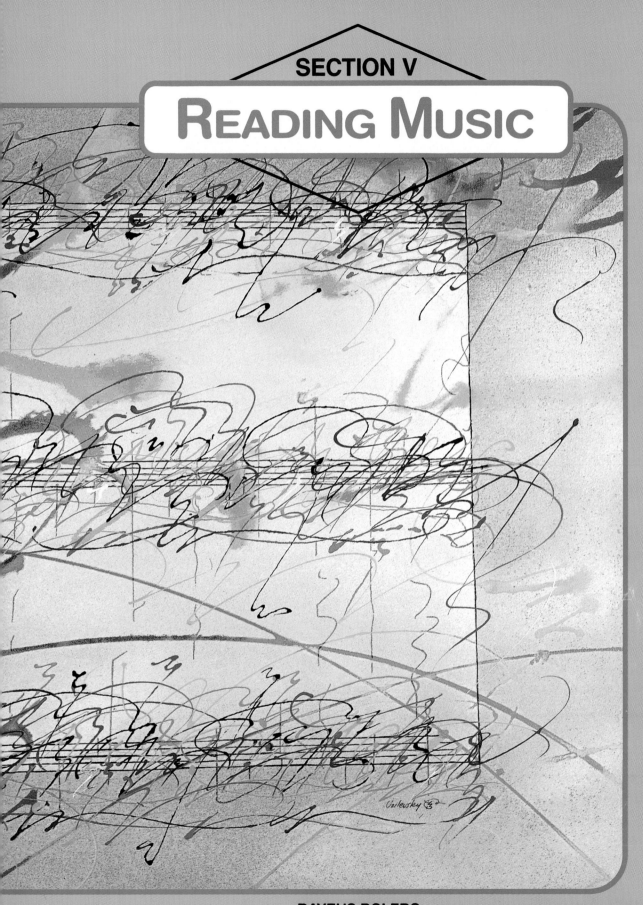

SECTION V

READING MUSIC

RAVEL'S BOLERO
Marcus Uzilevsky

A GHOST AND HIS TOAST

Miss White Had a Fright

Traditional

Miss White had a fright,

In the mid - dle of the night.

Saw a ghost eat - ing toast,

Half - way up the lamp - post.

la

so

mi

so mi so so mi

so so mi mi so so mi

so so la so so mi

so so la la so mi

230 UNIT 1 Focus on *so*, *mi*, *la*, and *do*

SINGING *LA*, *SO*, AND *MI*

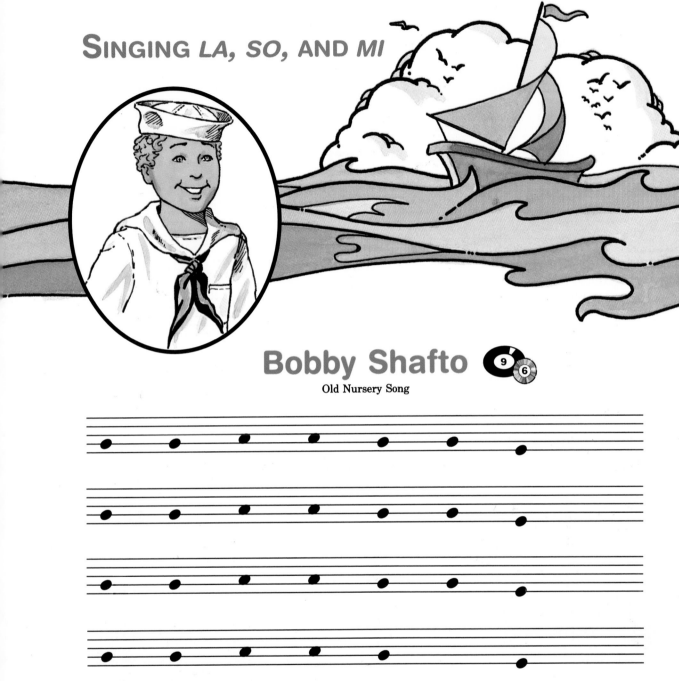

Bobby Shafto

Old Nursery Song

la

so

mi

SINGING *SO, MI,* AND *LA*

Rain, Rain

Street Rhyme

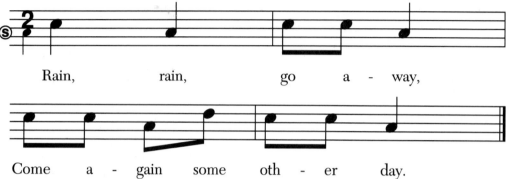

Rain,   rain,   go   a - way,

Come   a - gain   some   oth - er   day.

so   mi   so   la   so   mi   la
so _____

so   la   mi   la   so   la   mi
so _____

Hunt the Cows

MOTIVES WITH *SO-MI-DO*

What song is this?

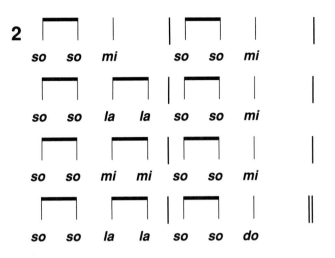

2

so so mi   so so mi

so so la la so so mi

so so mi mi so so mi

so so la la so so do

How many motives are in the song "Apple Tree"?

Are any of the motives exactly alike?

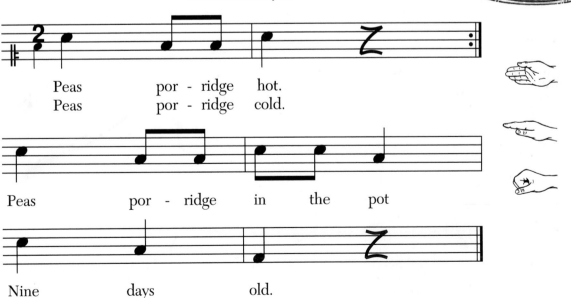

Peas Porridge Hot

Mother Goose Rhyme

Peas   por - ridge   hot.
Peas   por - ridge   cold.

Peas   por - ridge   in   the   pot

Nine   days   old.

MOTIVES AND PHRASES

● "Bounce High" as Two Motives

Bounce High, Bounce Low

Traditional

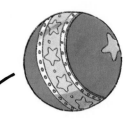

Bounce   high,   bounce   low,

Bounce   the   ball   to   Shi - loh!

Show the motives as you sing "Bounce High."
Pat the beat on your legs as you sing
"Bounce High" using rhythm syllables.
How many beats are in each motive?

● "Bounce High" as One Phrase

Bounce   high,   bounce   low,   Bounce the ball to Shi - loh!

Show the phrase in the air with your
hand as you sing.
How many beats are in this phrase?
How many phrases are in "Bounce High"?
How many motives are in "Bounce High"?

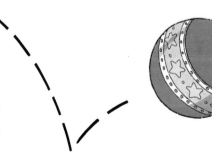

MOTIVES INTO PHRASES

I Won't Be My Father's Jack

Traditional   Collected and Adapted by Jean Sinor

I won't be my fa - ther's Jack,
I won't be my mo - ther's Jill,

I will be the fid - dler's wife,
And have mu - sic all my life.

The Millwheel

Traditional   Collected and Adapted by Katalin Forrai and Jean Sinor

'Round and 'round the wheel goes 'round,

as it turns the corn is ground.

Which song is written in motives?
Which song is written in phrases?

PHRASES AND OSTINATOS

Mouse, Mousie

Traditional

Mouse, mous-ie, Lit-tle mous-ie, hur — ry hur-ry do.

Or the kit-ty in her hous-ie will be chas-ing you!

● **A | Z Ostinato**

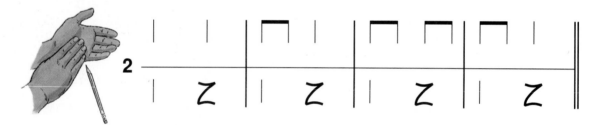

Can you make up a different two-beat ostinato?

Clap your ostinato as you sing "Mouse, Mousie."

What song is this?

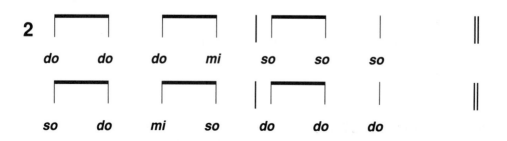

do do do mi so so so

so do mi so do do do

THE TIE

How many sounds are in ?

How many beats are in ?

Let's read the ties in
"Three Little Birdies."
Don't forget the repeat signs.

Three Little Birdies

Original Music by Lucille Wood   English Lyrics by Alice Firgau

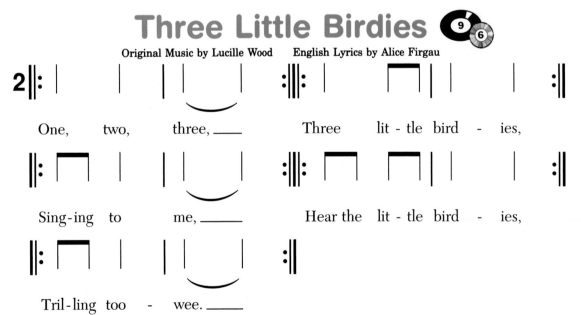

One,   two,   three, ____   Three   lit - tle bird - ies,

Sing-ing   to   me, ____   Hear the lit - tle bird - ies,

Tril-ling too - wee. ____

The Tie and the Half Note UNIT 3 **237**

THE TIE—ONE SOUND

One sound that lasts for 2 beats

Let's practice reading and clapping ♩.

Who's That Tapping at the Window?

American Folk Song   New Verses by Jill Trinka

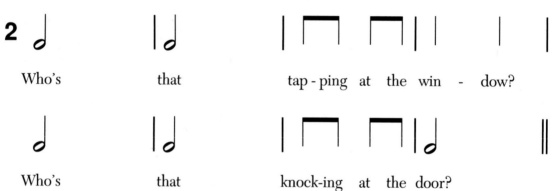

Who's   that   tap - ping   at   the   win - dow?

Who's   that   knock-ing   at   the   door?

What song is this?

READING *SO, MI,* AND A LONG *DO*

Can you guess what song this is?

so mi do mi do mi so

do _____

so la so mi so so do

do _____

I See the Moon

Traditional   Words by Earl Rogers

I   see the moon   and the moon   sees   me;

God   bless the moon   and may God   bless   me.

From LET'S SING TOGETHER by Denise Bacon. © 1971 by Boosey & Hawkes.

FORM

Can you clap the rhythm
of these words?

Rocky Mountain

Southern Folk Song

1. Rocky mountain, rocky mountain,
   rocky mountain high;
   When you're on that rocky mountain,
   hang your head and cry!

   Refrain:
   Do, do, do, do, Do remember me;
   Do, do, do, do, Do remember me.

2. Sunny valley, sunny valley,
   sunny valley low;
   When you're in that sunny valley,
   sing it soft and slow.

   Refrain:
   Do, do, do, do, Do remember me;
   Do, do, do, do, Do remember me.

3. Stormy ocean, stormy ocean,
   stormy ocean wide;
   When you're on that deep blue sea,
   There's no place you can hide.

   Refrain:
   Do, do, do, do, Do remember me;
   Do, do, do, do, Do remember me.

A New Sound

Let's find the new sound in songs we know.
Hum the new sound when you find it.

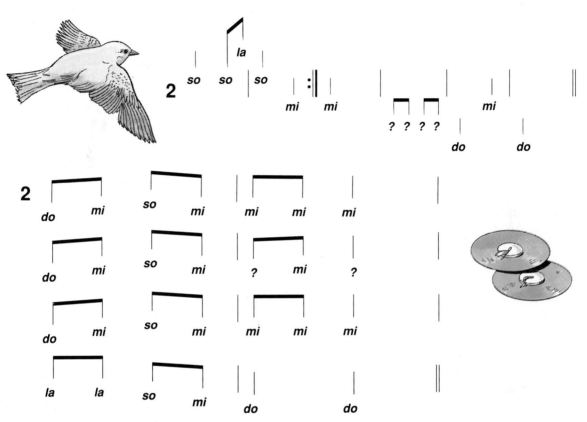

Rocky Mountain

Southern Folk Song

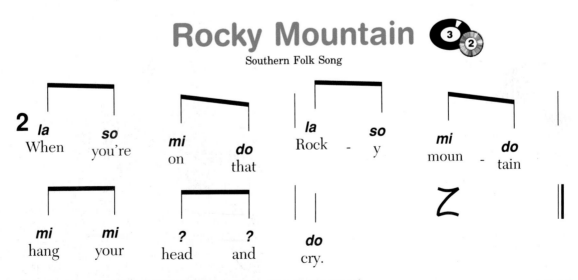

LEARNING ABOUT RE

The new sound between *mi* and *do* is called
$\boxed{re}$.

The *re* handsign looks like this:

re

Touch each word as you sing.
Sing the solfa and show the melody with
handsigns.

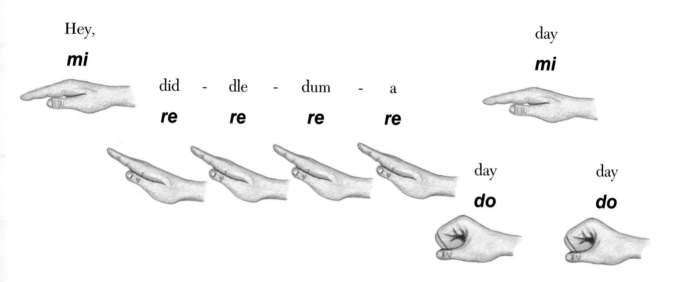

Hey,
mi

did - dle - dum - a
re **re** **re** **re**

day
mi

day
do

day
do

Do you know a song that starts like this?

FINDING *RE* ON THE STAFF

When *do* is in space 1:

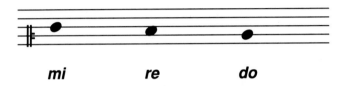

mi   re   do

When *do* is on line 2:

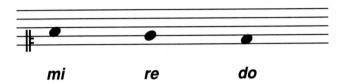

mi   re   do

When *do* is on the ledger line below the staff:

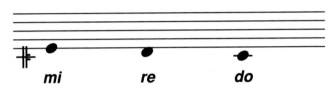

mi   re   do

● **Reading a *mi-re-do* Song on the Staff**

Hot Cross Buns

Folk Song from England

Hot   cross   buns,   hot   cross   buns,

one a pen - ny, two a pen - ny, hot   cross   buns.

On Halloween

Halloween, Halloween

Traditional

Hal-low-een,   Hal-low-een,   pump - kin   fat,

witch-es ride on broom - sticks,   wear-ing point-y hats.

Hal - low - een,   Hal - low - een,   big   black   cats!

LINES AND SPACES

Can you see that *mi* and *do* are in spaces?
Can you see that *re* will be on the line between
mi and *do*?

When *mi* and *do* are in spaces, *re* is always
on the line between them.

Pumpkin, Pumpkin

Traditional

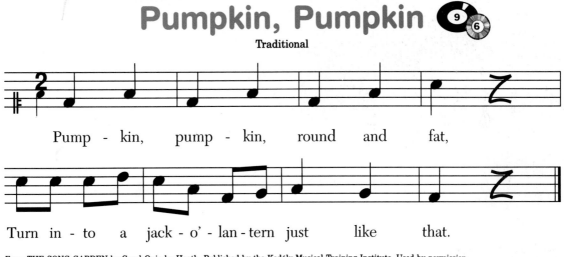

Pump - kin, pump - kin, round and fat,

Turn in - to a jack - o' - lan - tern just like that.

From THE SONG GARDEN by Carol Quimby Heath. Published by the Kodály Musical Training Institute. Used by permission.

When *mi* and *do* are on lines, *re* is always in
the space between them.

Pumpkin, Pumpkin

Traditional

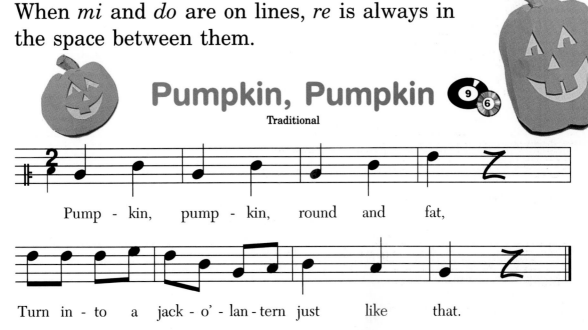

Pump - kin, pump - kin, round and fat,

Turn in - to a jack - o' - lan - tern just like that.

From THE SONG GARDEN by Carol Quimby Heath. Published by the Kodály Musical Training Institute. Used by permission.

How Do They Differ?

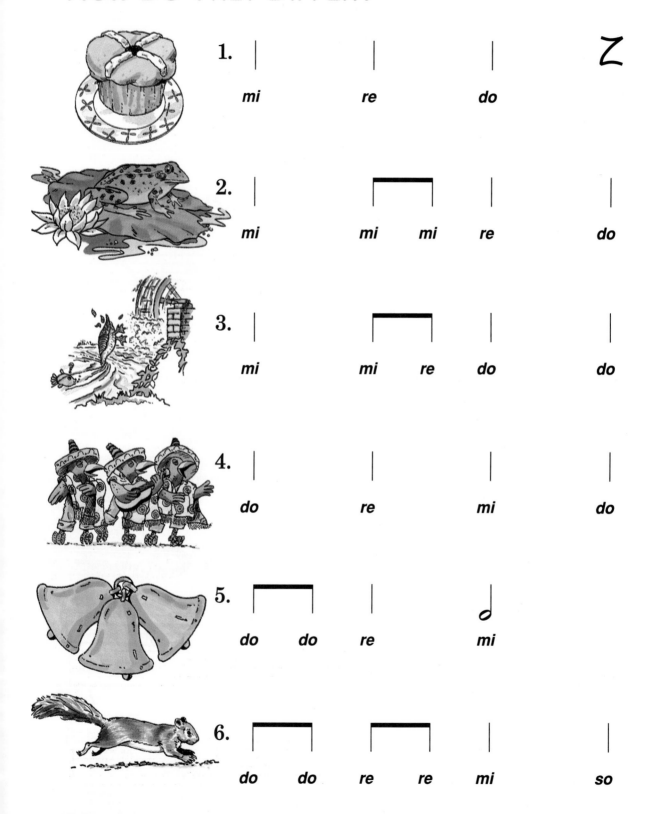

1. mi re do

2. mi mi mi re do

3. mi mi re do do

4. do re mi do

5. do do re mi

6. do do re re mi so

READING IN SOLFA

Let's read *mi*, *re*, and *do* in solfa.

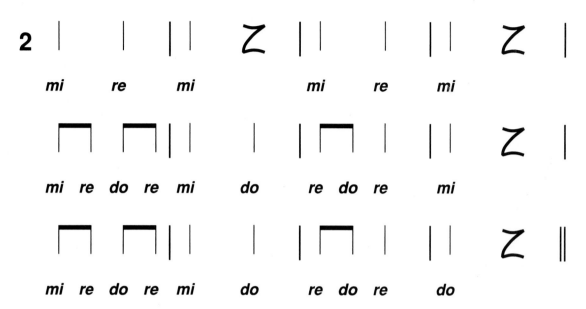

2

mi   re   mi   mi   re   mi

mi re do re mi   do   re do re   mi

mi re do re mi   do   re do re   do

mi

re

● Starting on *do*

do

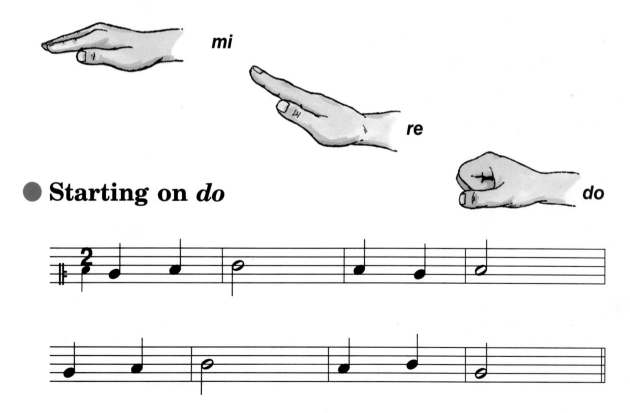

VERSE AND REFRAIN

The Open Plain

Traditional   Words by William Littlebear

VERSE:

On the o - pen plain, Buf - fa - lo, buf - fa - lo,

Hear the thund-'ring herd, Buf - fa - lo, buf - fa - lo.

REFRAIN:

Hi - yo   Hi - yo

Each verse has different words. The words of the refrain stay the same.

Play this ostinato with rattles as you sing "The Open Plain."

What song is this?

mi mi mi re do   re

so   mi   do

THE *SO-MI-RE-DO* FAMILY

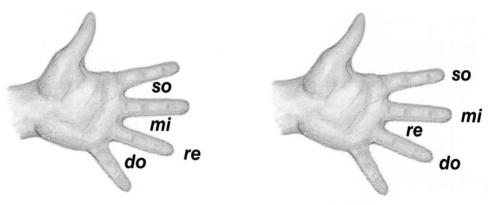

Show "Frosty Weather" on your hand

- starting with third space *so*.
- starting with fourth line *so*.

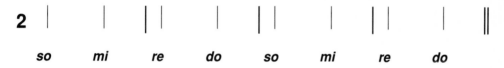

2 | | | | | | | | | | | ‖

so   *mi*   *re*   *do*   *so*   *mi*   *re*   *do*

Let Us Chase the Squirrel

Words and Music by Annie L. Preston

1. Let us chase the squir - rel, Up the hick - 'ry, down the hick - 'ry,

Let us chase the squir - rel, Up the hick - 'ry tree.

How are the first two measures of "Frosty Weather" and "Let Us Chase the Squirrel" different?

How are they alike?

You Are Eating, Drinking

Traditional Hungarian Folk Song

You are eat - ing, drink - ing,

But you don't in - vite me,

It's not nice!

Can you clap this ostinato as you sing the song again?

Let's use *so-do* to sing a melodic ostinato for this song.

so so so do
Not ver-y nice!

READING *DO, MI, RE* AND *SO*

Sammy Sackett

Dutch Folk Song   English Words by Mary Tolbert

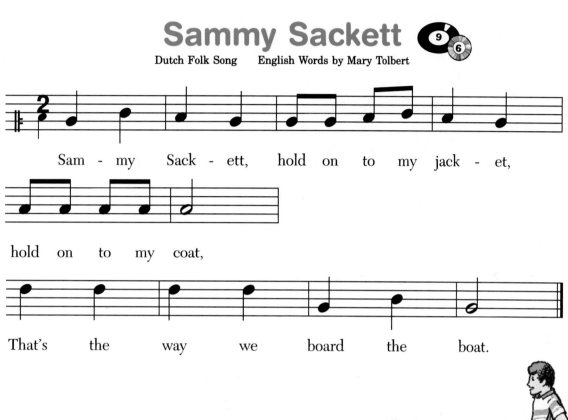

Sam - my Sack - ett, hold on to my jack - et,

hold on to my coat,

That's the way we board the boat.

Let's read a new song with *so, mi, re,* and *do.*

Hey, Hop Along

Traditional

Hey, Hop a - long, Hop a - long, Jo - sey,

Hey, Hop a - long, Hop a - long, Joe.

Something About Form **251**

OSTINATOS ON *SO* AND *DO*

Who's That Tapping at the Window?

American Folk Song   New Verses by Jill Trinka

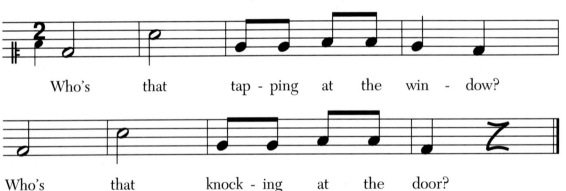

Who's   that   tap - ping   at   the   win - dow?

Who's   that   knock - ing   at   the   door?

Copyright 1925 by Harvard University Press; 1953 by Mary McDaniel Parker

Sing this ostinato for "Who's That Tapping?"

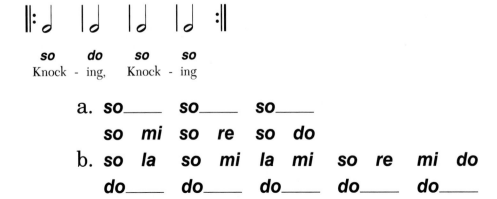

so   *do*   *so*   *so*
Knock - ing,   Knock - ing

a. *so____   so____   so____*
   so   mi   so   re   so   do

b. *so   la   so   mi   la   mi   so   re   mi   do*
   do____   do____   do____   do____   do____

Christmas Day Is Come

Traditional Irish Carol

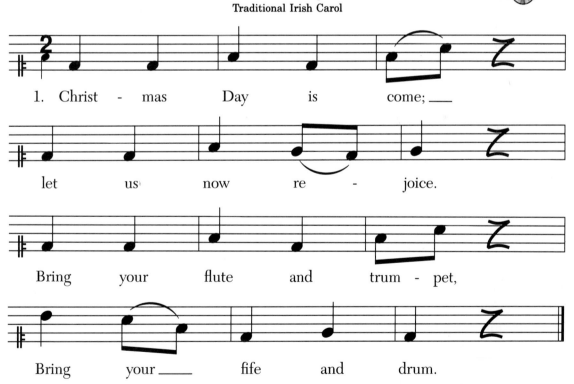

1. Christ - mas Day is come; ___

let us now re - joice.

Bring your flute and trum - pet,

Bring your ___ fife and drum.

Clap this ostinato as you sing.

WHERE IS THE OSTINATO?

Can you find a rhythmic ostinato on this page?

Santa's Arrival

Music by Zoltan Kodály

do re mi so la

All the world is dressed in white,

fin - ger tips are ting - ling;

Fath - er Christ - mas comes to - night,

Rein - deer bells are jing - ling.

From FIFTY NURSERY SONGS. Copyright © 1942 by Boosey & Hawkes Music Publishers Ltd. Copyright renewed. Reprinted by permission of Boosey & Hawkes Inc.

2. Soon across the lake he'll go,
   on his sleigh a-riding,
   Speeding over ice and snow,
   hear the runners gliding.

3. Crackling logs and mistletoe,
   red the holly berry,
   Santa Claus is coming here,
   red his face and merry.

4. Welcome then, dear Santa Claus,
   welcome then and rightly,
   Rest your star upon our tree,
   so it shines out brightly.

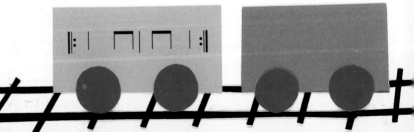

HOLIDAY MORNING

REVIEWING *MI-RE-DO*

Who's That Yonder?

African-American Spiritual

Who's that yon - der dressed in red?

Must be the chil - dren that Mo - ses led.

2. Who's that yonder dressed in white?
   Must be the people of the Israelites.

3. Who's that yonder dressed in green?
   Must be Ezekiel in his flyin' machine.

4. Who's that yonder dressed in blue?
   Must be the children that are comin' through.

5. Who's that yonder dressed in black?
   Must be the people that are comin' back.

How does the melody end?

Hold the *do* as your teacher sings the upper-voice solfa.

mi do mi do mi re do
do _____

Switch parts.

Now hold *so*:

so _____
mi do mi re mi re do

Switch parts.

USING LEDGER LINE *DO*

Suo Gan

Welsh Lullaby   **English Words by J. Trinka**

Su - o gan, do not weep,

Su - o gan, go to sleep,

Su - o gan, Moth - er's near,

Su - o gan, have no fear.

What do you notice about the rhythm of each line?

How does the melody for each line begin?

Does the melody for each line end the same?

Which lines have the same ending?

What is the form of "Suo Gan"?

SING AND TAP

When I'm Dancing

English Words by Patricia Brewer   Music by Zoltán Kodály

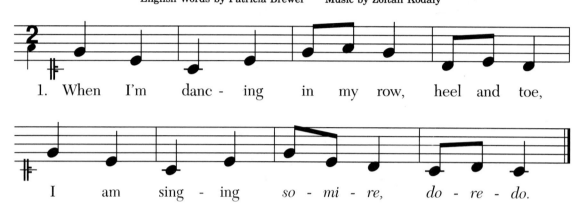

1. When I'm danc-ing in my row, heel and toe,
I am sing-ing *so - mi - re,* *do - re - do.*

2. Dance together one by one, two by two.
When the music calls to me, calls to you.

Tap the rhythm of the bottom part as you sing
the top part.

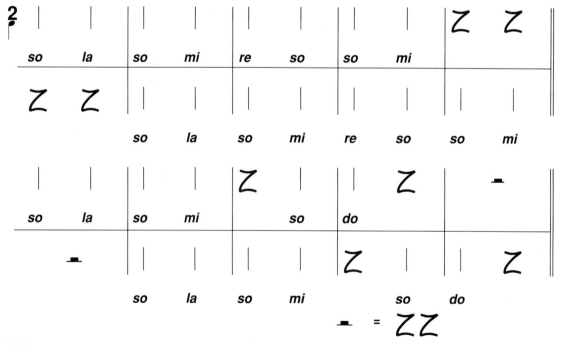

258   Ledger Line *do*

How Does It End?

All Around the Buttercup

Traditional Singing Game

1.

All a - round the but - ter cup, one, two, three.
If you want a nice young friend,

2.

just choose me.

From LET'S SING TOGETHER, (Bacon), Published by
Boosey & Hawkes © 1971

Bye, Bye, Baby

Appalachian Lullaby

1.

Bye, bye, ___ ba - by, ba - by, bye,
My lit - tle ba - by,

2.

ba - by, bye.

From ENGLISH FOLK SONGS collected by Cecil Sharp. Courtesy of Oxford University Press.

THE REFRAIN

Fiddle-Dee-Dee

Folk Song from England

REFRAIN

Fid - dle - dee - dee, Fid - dle - dee - dee,

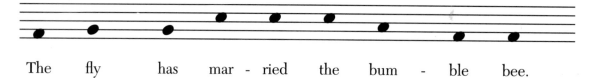

The fly has mar - ried the bum - ble bee.

1. Says the fly, says he, "Will you marry me,
   And live with me, sweet bumblebee?" *Refrain*

2. Says the bee, says she, "I'll live under your wing,
   And you'll never know that I carry a sting." *Refrain*

3. So when the parson had joined the pair,
   They both went out to take the air. *Refrain*

4. And the flies did buzz and the bells did ring,
   Did you ever hear so merry a thing? *Refrain*

5. And then to think that of all the flies,
   The bumblebee should carry the prize. *Refrain*

My Dog Sings in Solfa

Bow Wow Wow

Traditional Nursery Song

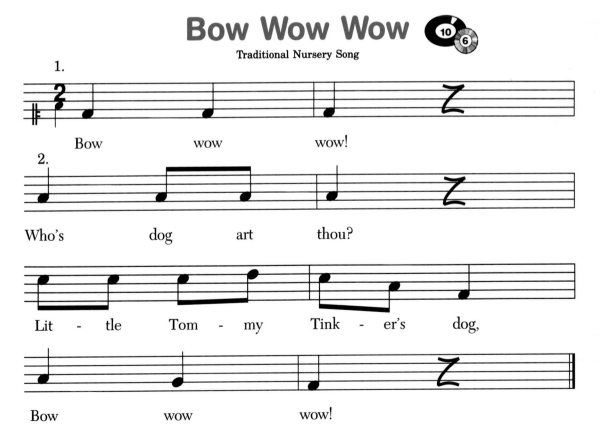

1.
Bow wow wow!

2.
Who's dog art thou?

Lit - tle Tom - my Tink - er's dog,

Bow wow wow!

LIKE AND UNLIKE PHRASES

Teddy Bear

Jump Rope Chant

do re mi so la

Ted - dy Bear, Ted - dy Bear, turn a - round, ___
Ted - dy Bear, Ted - dy Bear, show your shoe, ___

Ted - dy Bear, Ted - dy Bear, touch the ground,
Ted - dy Bear, Ted - dy Bear, that will do!

Ted - dy Bear, Ted - dy Bear, go up stairs, ___

Ted - dy Bear, Ted - dy Bear, say your prayers.

Ted - dy Bear, Ted - dy Bear, turn off the light,

Ted - dy Bear, Ted - dy Bear, say Good - night!

How many phrases are there in "Teddy Bear"?
Which phrases are exactly alike?

A VERY TALL HOUSE

Great Big House

Folk Song from Louisiana

Great big house in New Or - leans,

For - ty sto - ries high; _____

Ev - 'ry room that I been in,

Filled with pump - kin pie.

2. Went down to the old mill stream,
   To fetch a pail of water;
   Put one arm around my wife,
   The other 'round my daughter.

3. Fare thee well, my darling girl,
   Fare thee well, my daughter;
   Fare thee well, my darling girl,
   With the golden slippers on her.

LOUD AND SOFT

Firefly

Japanese Folk Song
English Version by Katherine S. Bolt, Edith Krohnet, and Jill Trinka

Fire - fly, fire - fly, in the night.

With a yel - low, with a yel - low, with a yel - low light,

How I like to watch you shine to - night.

2. Firefly, firefly, may I speak?
Did you turn your light out, are you playing hide and seek?
Up among the trees I see you peek.

3. Firefly, firefly, please don't go,
Will you take me with you, I would like to fly, you know,
Up above the trees, I'd love it so.

Clap this ostinato lightly as you sing.
Which sound has more energy than other sounds?
Now clap the ostinato again, but this time clap it louder.

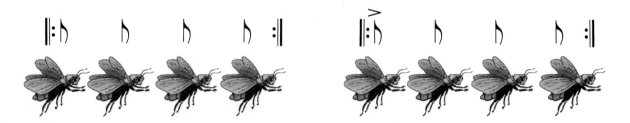

Rocky Mountain

Southern Folk Song

Rock-y moun-tain, rock-y moun-tain, rock-y moun-tain high;

When you're on that rock-y moun-tain, hang your head and cry!

REFRAIN

Do, do, do, do, Do re - mem - ber me;

Do, do, do, do, Do re - mem - ber me.

2. Sunny valley, sunny valley,
sunny valley low,
When you're in that sunny valley,
sing it soft and slow. *Chorus*

3. Stormy ocean, stormy ocean,
stormy ocean wide,
When you're on that deep blue sea,
There's no place you can hide.
Chorus

A Duet

Button, You Must Wander

Traditional Game Song

I

But - ton, you must wan - der, wan - der, wan - der,

II

Wan - der, But - ton,

I

But - ton, you must wan - der ev - 'ry - where;

II

Wan - der, But - ton;

I

Bright eyes will find you, sharp eyes will find you,

II

Bright eyes find you,

I

But - ton, you must wan - der ev - 'ry - where.

II

Wan - der, But - ton!

A Jazzy Little Rhythm

Somebody Loves Me

Words and Music by Gaynor Jones

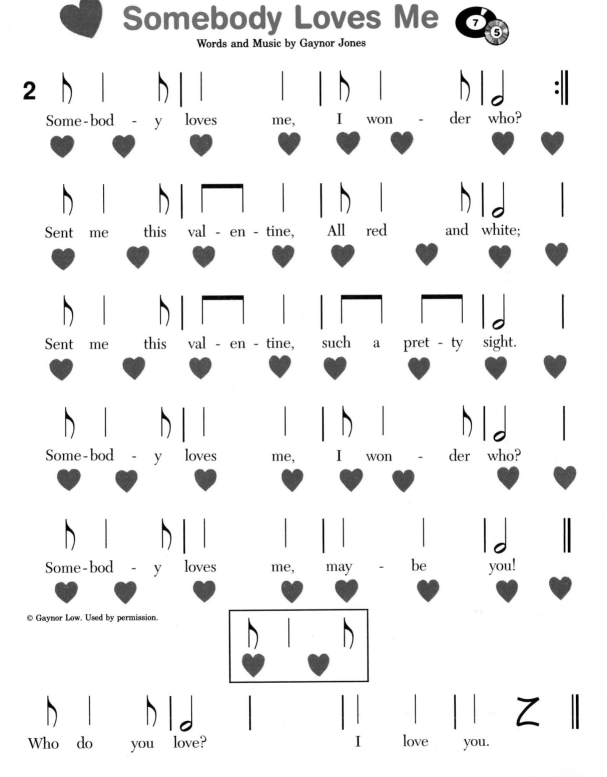

Some-bod - y loves me, I won - der who?

Sent me this val - en - tine, All red and white;

Sent me this val - en - tine, such a pret - ty sight.

Some-bod - y loves me, I won - der who?

Some-bod - y loves me, may - be you!

© Gaynor Low. Used by permission.

Who do you love? I love you.

RHYTHMIC FORM

Leila
Folk Song from North Carolina

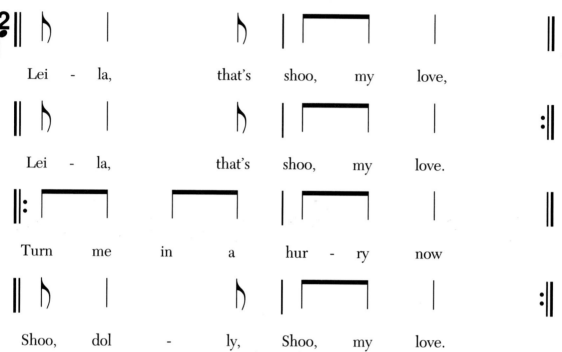

Lei - la,   that's   shoo,   my   love,

Lei - la,   that's   shoo,   my   love.

Turn   me   in   a   hur - ry   now

Shoo,   dol - ly,   Shoo,   my   love.

Look at the symbols ◯ and △.

Each stands for two measures of the song.
Which is the best picture of the rhythmic form
of "Leila"?

1. ◯ ◯ △ ◯ △ ◯ ◯ ◯

2. ◯ △ ◯ △ ◯ △ ◯ △

3. ◯ ◯ ◯ ◯ △ ◯ △ ◯

BEATS GROUPED IN 2

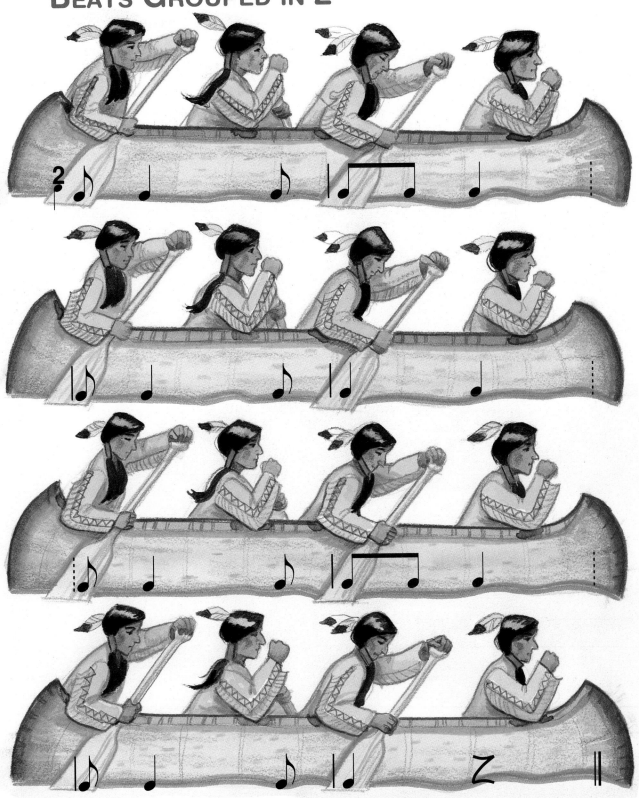

MAKING MUSIC

We Like Music

Traditional

1. We like mu - sic!

We like mu - sic, one turn ___ a - round now.

2. We like singing!
   We like singing,
   One turn around now.

3. We like moving!
   We like moving,
   One turn around now.

Make up other verses for things you like to

eat   smell   touch   see.

● **A Two-part Rhythm with** ♪ | ♪

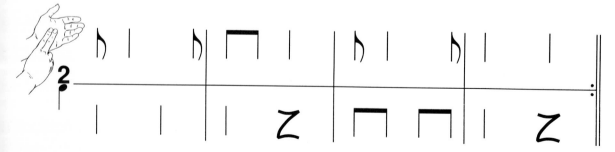

MAKING UP VERSES

Dog and Cat 🔟6️⃣

Folk Song from South Carolina

VERSE

1. *Bought* me a *dog, bought* me a *cat,*
   They both *fight* but *do* not *mind* that,

REFRAIN

Hi - ho,   my   dar - lin'.

2. Bought me a 🧥, bought me a 🧢 ,
   They don't fit but do not mind that,
   Hi-ho, my darlin'.

3. Bought me a ⚾, bought me a 🏏 ,
   They don't work but do not mind that,
   Hi-ho, my darlin'.

4. Bought me a 🐁 , bought me a 🐈 ,
   They both squeak but do not mind that,
   Hi-ho, my darlin'.

From FOLK SONGS OF THE SOUTHERN APPALACHIANS by Cecil Sharp. Used
courtesy of Oxford University Press.

Some children in New Haven,
Connecticut made up verses
three and four.

Can you make up some more verses?

ANOTHER SONG ABOUT NOAH

Old Ark

American Spiritual

VERSE

1. Old Ark she roll, Old Ark she rock,

Old Ark a-sit-tin' on the moun-tain top.

REFRAIN

Old Ark a-mov-in', mov-in', child-ren won't you come a-long,

Old Ark a-mov-in', I thank God.

Old Ark she reel, Old Ark she rock,

Old Ark a-sit-tin' on the moun-tain top!

2. God called Noah from the mountain top,
   Command Old Noah to build his ark.

3. God told Noah by the rainbow sign,
   No more water but fire next time.

A RHYTHM DUET

Clap the bottom rhythm as you sing.

A Pretty Girl
Una Muchacha
Folk Song from Puerto Rico

2

Give me a girl and then a gui - tar and
U - na mu - cha - cha, u - na gui - tar - ra,

then I can sing my song, oh!
pa - ra po - der can - tar, ¡ay!

Give me a girl and then a gui - tar and
U - na mu - cha - cha, u - na gui - tar - ra,

then I can sing my song, oh!
pa - ra po - der can - tar, ¡ay!

THE WHOLE NOTE

$\boxed{\mathbf{o}}$ = One sound that lasts for four beats.

Hush, Hush

Traditional Spiritual

1. Hush, hush, some-bod - y's call - in' my name;

2. Hush, hush, some-bod - y's call - in' my name;

3. Hush, hush, some-bod - y's call - in' my name;

4. Hush, hush, some-bod - y's call - in' my name.

2. Who, who, who Lord is callin' my name?   *(4 times)*

3. You, you, you Lord are callin' my name.   *(4 times)*

From LET'S SING TOGETHER by Denise Bacon. © Boosey and Hawkes, 1972

$\boxed{\begin{smallmatrix} 4 \\ \text{♩} \end{smallmatrix}}$ = Four beats in each measure.

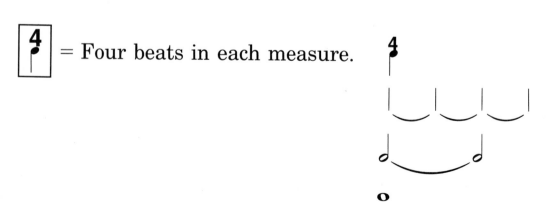

CONDUCTING IN 4

Conduct as you sing.

Come Out Tonight
Folk Song from Alabama

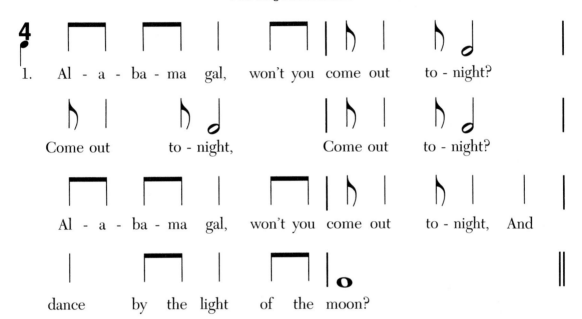

1. Al - a - ba - ma gal, won't you come out to - night?

Come out to - night, Come out to - night?

Al - a - ba - ma gal, won't you come out to - night, And

dance by the light of the moon?

2. Mississippi gal, won't you come out tonight, . . .

3. California gal, won't you come out tonight, . . .

4. South Dakota gal, won't you come out tonight, . . .

What state do you live in?
Sing about your state.

What states are next to your state?
Sing about them, too.

SINGING IN CANON

One Jar

Hungarian Folk Song
Words by Patricia Brewer
Adapted by Jill Trinka

One jar of ap - ples,   Three jars of ap - ples,
Two jars of ap - ples,   Four jars of ap - ples,

Five jars of ap - ples,   Se - ven jars of ap - ples,
Six jars of ap - ples,

Eight jars of ap - ples,   Nine jars of ap - ples,

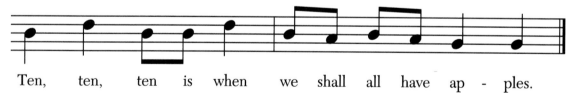

Ten, ten, ten is when we shall all have ap - ples.

2. One jar of pickles,
   Two jars of pickles, . . .

What would you like your jar
to be filled with?
Let's sing in canon.

Hear the Birds

These birds can sing in Spanish. Sing the song in English, then try to sing it in Spanish.

Three Little Birdies
Tres Pajarillos

Words and Music by Lucille Wood   English Lyrics by Alica Firgau

One, two, three,   One, two, three,
Uno,   dos,   tres,   *Uno,   dos,   tres,*

Three lit - tle bird - ies,   Three lit - tle bird - ies,
Tres   pa - ja - ri - llos,   *tres   pa - ja - ri - llos,*

Sing - ing to me,   sing - ing to me.
Can - tan   a - sí,   *can - tan   a - sí,*

Hear the lit - tle bird - ies,   hear the lit - tle bird - ies,
Pi - pa - rí - a - rí - a,   *pi - pa - rí - a - rí - a,*

Tril - ling too - wee,   tril - ling too - wee.
Can - tan   a - sí,   *can - tan   a - sí.*

A SNAKE IN THE BUSH

Black Snake

Traditional

Black snake, black snake, where are you hi - ding?

Black snake, black snake, where are you hi - ding?

Black snake, black snake, where are you hi - ding?

Don't you bite _____ me!

Who Did It?

Use the four-beat conducting pattern as you sing the first verse.

Is there a **o** in this song?

Does it occur at the beginning, in the middle, or at the end of the song?

The Death of the Robin
American Folk Song

1. Who killed the Robin?
   Who killed the Robin?
   "I," said the sparrow,
   "with my little bow and arrow,
   It was I, oh, it was I."

2. Who saw him die?
   Who saw him die?
   "I," said the fly,
   "with my little teeny eye,
   It was I, oh, it was I."

3. Who dug his grave?
   Who dug his grave?
   "I," said the crow,
   "with my little spade and hoe,
   It was I, oh, it was I."

4. Who sang his funeral?
   Who sang his funeral?
   "I," said the lark,
   "with a song and with a harp,
   It was I, oh, it was I."

A BIT OF JAPAN

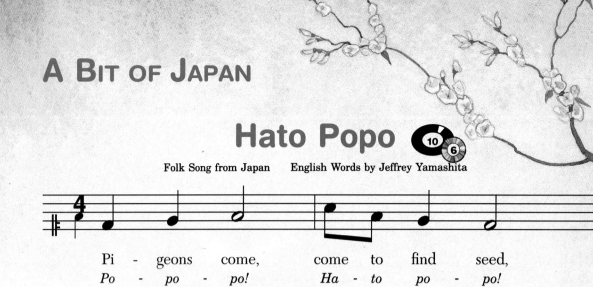

Hato Popo

Folk Song from Japan   English Words by Jeffrey Yamashita

Pi - geons come,   come to find seed,
Po - po - po!   Ha - to po - po!

So   I   will spread the grains of mil - let for their feed.
Ma - me ga ho - shi - i - ka? So - ra ya - ru zo!

Come,   love - ly pi - geons, take the mil - let for your need.
Mi - na - de na - ka - yo - ku, Ta - be - ni ko - i.

ANOTHER NEW SOUND

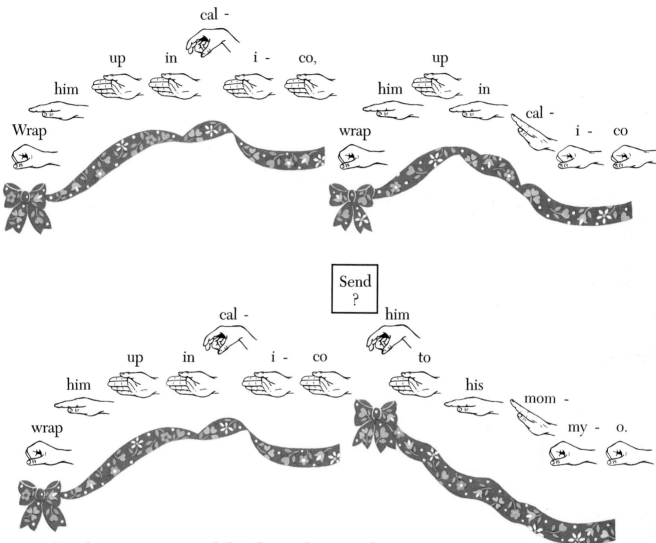

Is the new sound higher than *so*?
Is it higher than *la*?
Does it sound like any other sound we know?

HIGH DO

The name of the new sound is high *do*.
High *do* has the same handsign as *do*.
There is something different about high *do*.
Can you tell what it is?

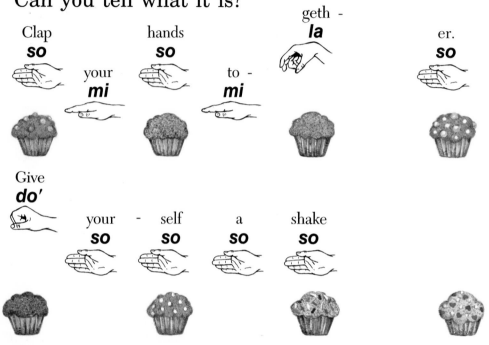

We use a tick (') to show the difference between
do and high *do*: $\boxed{do'}$ tells us to sing high *do*.

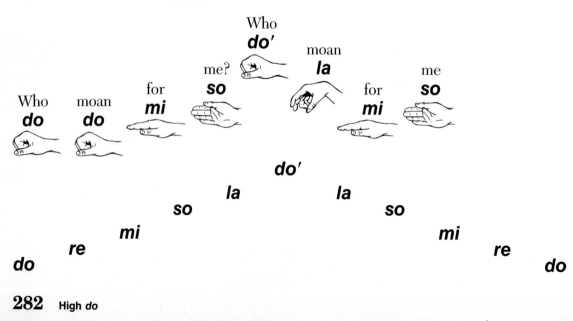

282   High *do*

High *do* (*d'*) on the Staff

Can you find high do on the staff?

Can you find *do'* in this song?

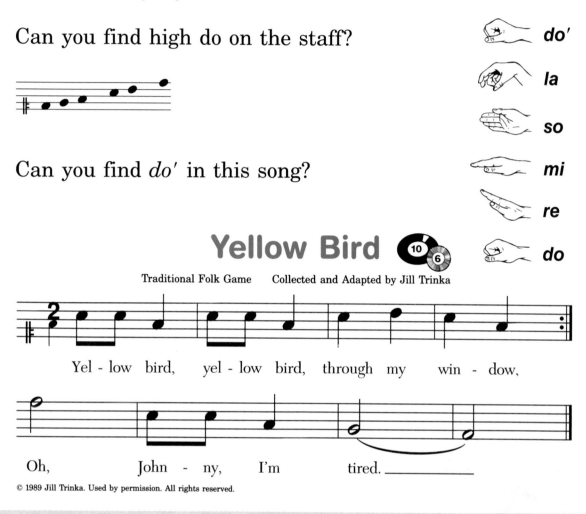

Yellow Bird

Traditional Folk Game   Collected and Adapted by Jill Trinka

Yel - low bird,   yel - low bird,   through my   win - dow,

Oh,   John - ny,   I'm   tired. _____

do mi so mi so la so
do _____

so la do' la do' la so
do _____

so do' so mi re so do
do _____

ANOTHER HOME FOR HIGH *DO*

I Want to Be a Farmer

Ohio Play Party Song

VERSE

I want to be a farmer, a farmer, a farmer,
I want to be a farmer, and by my lady stand.
With a pitch fork on my shoulder, my shoulder, my shoulder,
With a pitch fork on my shoulder, and a sickle in my hand.

REFRAIN

Bow la - dies bow, gents, you know how,
All prom - en - ade, all prom - en - ade,

Swing that left hand la - dy round, all prom - en - ade.

FAST AND SLOW

Clocks

Traditional Danish Three-part Round English Words by Polly Carder

1.

Great big clocks go tick - tock, tick - tock.

2.

While the smal-ler man-tle clocks go tick-tock, tick-tock, tick-tock, tick-tock,

3.

And the shin - y lit - tle watch-es keep on work-ing day and night with

tick - y, tock - y, tick - y, tock - y, tick - y, tock - y, tick.

From *Brownie's Own Songbook* (selected and compiled by Ann Roos and Alicen White) Roos and Coe-White Associates, 220 East 19th Street, New York, N.Y. 10003, © 1968

High *do*

A NEW SONG WITH *DO'*

Here is a new song to sing.
It uses high *do*.

Peas in the Pot

Folk Song from North Carolina

Peas in the pot   Hoe - cake a - ba - kin';

Sal - ly in the kitch - en with her shirt - tail a - sha - kin'.

From COLLECTION OF NORTH CAROLINA FOLKLORE by Frank C. Brown. Used by permission of Duke University Press.

Can you sing this song using solfa syllables?

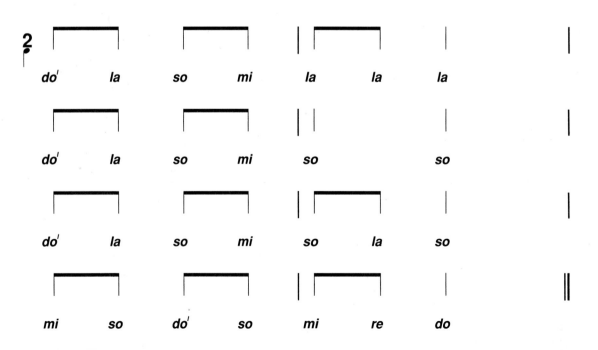

do' la so mi la la la

do' la so mi so so

do' la so mi so la so

mi so do' so mi re do

Using High *do*

Dancing Song
Traditional

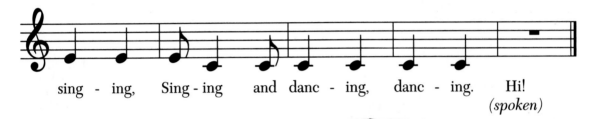

Danc-ing and sing - ing, Danc-ing and sing - ing, Danc-ing and

sing - ing, Sing - ing and danc - ing, danc - ing. Hi!
(spoken)

You know the names of six different pitches or tones. From the lowest pitch to the highest pitch they are:

do   re   mi   so   la   do'

Which pitch is *not* used in "Dancing Song"?

Sing this ostinato.

danc-ing, sing-ing, danc-ing, sing-ing.

ELEMENTARY, MY DEAR WATSON

Mystery Song

Words and Music by Gaynor Jones

© Gaynor Low. Used by permission.

Do You Know These Songs?

The Sound Bank

String Instruments

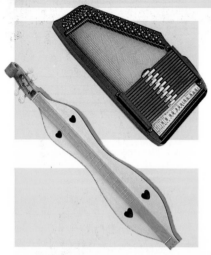

Autoharp   A soundbox with strings across it. When a chord button is pressed, only the strings that fit the chord will sound. We can strum the strings to make sounds that will go with a song.

Dulcimer   A soundbox with strings across it. The strings are usually plucked with a quill. The sound is quiet and sweet.

Guitar   A string instrument plucked with fingers or a pick. A guitar can play a melody. It can also make chords to accompany a melody. Some guitars are electric. They can sound much louder than a regular guitar. They can also make many special sounds.

Violin   A string instrument that is usually played with a bow. It can also be plucked. The violin plays sounds from low to very high. It can make many different kinds of sounds.

Wind Instruments

Flute   A wind instrument shaped like a metal pipe. The player holds the flute sideways and blows across a mouthpiece. The flute can make high sounds.

Piccolo   A very small flute. It can make sounds that are higher than the flute.

Keyboard Instruments

Piano A large keyboard instrument with strings inside. When we press the keys, hammers inside the piano hit the strings and make them sound. Some people have a piano in their house. You may have a piano in your school.

Synthesizer An "electronic" instrument with a keyboard like a piano. It uses electricity in a special way to make sounds. The synthesizer can make many kinds of sounds, even imitate other instruments.

Classroom Percussion Instruments

Bells Metal bars that ring when struck with a mallet. Bells come in different sizes to play higher and lower sounds.

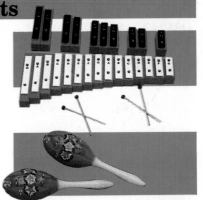

Maracas Large round "rattles" with handles. Shaking the maracas makes a crisp "swishing" sound.

Tambourine A round instrument with small metal discs around the edge. Shaking or hitting the tambourine makes a jingling sound.

Woodblock A hollow wooden bar that is hit with a mallet. It can make a ticking or popping sound. Woodblocks of different sizes make higher or lower sounds.

GLOSSARY

ABA form *(p. 120)* A musical plan that has three parts, or sections. The first and last sections are the same. The middle section is different. "Shoo, Fly" *(p. 134)* is a song in **ABA form.**

bar, barline A vertical line drawn through a staff to separate measures. All the songs in your book have bar lines.

beat *(p. 64)* A repeating pulse that can be felt in some music. Pat the **beat** in your lap when you sing "Ev'rybody's Welcome" *(p. 4).*

do clef A symbol (𝄪) that is placed on a staff to show the position of *do.* You can see a *do* clef on p. 233.

downward *(p. 48)* Moving from a higher tone to a lower one. "In the Sea" *(p. 10)* ends with tones that move **downward.**

eighth notes *(p. 93)*—♫—*See* **note.**

even *(p. 101) See* **rhythm pattern.**

fast *(p. 60)* Moving quickly. *The Ball (p. 65)* is an example of music that is **fast.**

half note *(p. 93)*—♩—*See* **note.**

handsigns A way to show pitches by using different hand shapes. *(p. 231)*

high *(p. 60)* A sound notated near the top of the staff. "Do-Re-Mi" *(p. 82)* ends with a **high** sound.

introduction *(p. 79)* In a song, music played before the singing begins. Most songs on the music recordings begin with an instrumental **introduction.**

leap *(p. 85)* Moving from one tone to another, skipping over the tones in between. "It's Me!" *(p. 20)* begins with tones that **leap.**

long *(p. 60)* A sound that is not as short as others around it. *In the Hall of the Mountain King (p. 28)* begins with a **long** sound played on horns.

loud *(p. 60)* Not quiet. The music of *Invocation of the Powerful Spirits (p. 143)* is too **loud** to be a lullaby.

low *(p. 60)* A sound notated near the bottom of the staff. The verse of "Growing-Up Song" *(p. 46)* begins with **low** tones.

lullaby *(p. 108)* A quiet song, often sung when rocking a child to sleep. "Sleep, My Little Bird" *(p. 36)* is a **lullaby.**

measure A group of beats set off by barlines. *(p. 249)*

melody *(p. 103)* A line of single tones that move upward, downward, or repeat. The **melody** of "Old Dan Tucker" *(p. 116)* begins with tones that repeat.

mood *(p. 143)* The feeling that a piece of music gives. The **mood** of "Lullaby, My Jamie" *(p. 142)* is quiet and gentle.

motive A little bit of music, usually only a few notes long. **Motives** are put together to build phrases. *(p. 233)*

no beat *(p. 67)* Giving no feeling of a repeated pulse. Listen for the sections with **no beat** in *Moon Music (p. 67)*.

note *(p. 50)* A symbol for sound in music. You have learned about **eighth notes** (♪ ♪), the **quarter note** (♩), and the **half note** (♩).

phrase *(p. 50)* A musical "sentence" that expresses one musical thought. There are five **phrases** in "Who Has Seen the Wind?" *(p. 106)*.

quarter note *(p. 93)*—♩—See **note**.

repeated tones *(p. 84)* Two or more tones in a row that have the same sound. "Chumbara" *(p. 88)* begins with **repeated tones.**

rhythm pattern *(p. 101)* A grouping of long and short sounds. Some **rhythm patterns** have even sounds—♩ ♪♪ ♩ ♩

long short short long long

Other **rhythm patterns** have uneven sounds—♩ ♪ ♩ ♪

long short long short

score *(p. 102)* The printed music for a song or instrumental work. Follow the **score** on page 52 when you sing "Who Built the Ark?"

section *(p. 112)* A part of a song or instrumental work. "Scrapin' Up Sand" has two **sections**, A and B.

so clef A small circle with "s" in the center that is placed on a staff to show the position of *so*. *(p. 232)*

short *(p. 60)* A sound that is not as long as others around it. In *Polka (p. 102)* the xylophone melody has **short** sounds.

slow *(p. 60)* Not quick. In *The Swan (p. 107)* the cello plays a **slow** melody.

soft *(p. 60)* Quiet. We sing lullabies in a **soft** voice.

solfa The tone syllables used in reading music: *do-re-mi-fa-so-la-ti-do'*. *(p. 247)*

steady beat *(p. 64)* Regular pulses. Pat your lap to the **steady beat** when you sing your favorite song.

step *(p. 84)* Moving from one tone to another without skipping tones between. The verse of "Do-Re-Mi" *(p. 82)* ends with tones that **step** upward.

story song *(p. 18)* A song in which the words tell a story. "Mister Frog Went A-Courtin'" *(p. 18)* is a **story song.**

string instrument *(p. 72)* A musical instrument played by bowing, plucking, or strumming a string. A violin is a **string instrument.**

uneven *(p. 101)* See **rhythm pattern.**

upward *(p. 48)* Moving from a lower tone to a higher one. "How Old Are You?" *(p. 8)* begins with tones that move **upward.**

Classified Index

FOLK AND TRADITIONAL SONGS

HOLIDAY AND SPECIAL-OCCASION SONGS

LISTENING LIBRARY

POEMS

THEME MUSICAL

SONG INDEX

ACKNOWLEDGMENTS

Credit and appreciation are due the publisher and the copyright owner for use of the following.

"This Happy Day" from THE LITTLE HILL by Harry Behn. Copyright 1949 by Harry Behn. © renewed 1977 by Alice L. Behn. All rights reserved. Reprinted by permission of Marian Reiner.

PICTURE CREDITS

Contributing Artists: Christa Keiffer 2, 3, 96, 97, 106, 140, 141, 166, 167, 202, 211; Michelle Noiset 7, 18, 19, 30, 31, 98, 99, 104, 105, 137, 158, 159, 200, 201, 208, 209, 218, 219; Joe Veno 12, 41, 50, 100, 278, 279; Nancy Munger 17, 269, 273, 287; Stephen Moscowitz 22, 23, 172, 173; Gail Roth 26, 54, 180, 181, 182, 184–188, 190–193; Katherine Ace 27; Fred Marvin 28, 29, 118, 119; Laurie Jordan 49, 51, 162, 165, 170, 171, 196, 197, 214, 215, 223, 252, 253; Mary Bausman 52, 53, 60, 69, 95, 117, 168, 169; Eulala Connor 56, 57, 102, 123, 130, 157, 178, 179, 206; Patti Boyd 58, 59; David Wisniewski 101, 103, 120, 177, 198, 199, 220, 221; Julie Durrell 110, 111; Susan Spellman 113, 259; Wendy Rasmusseu 142, 143, 231, 232, 242, 247, 249, 257, 270; Michael Adams 155; Bob Barner 216, 222, 244, 245; Tom Cardamone 230–239, 241, 243, 246, 248, 251, 256, 261, 262, 264, 277, 286; Lois Ehlert 254, 255; Fred Daunno 260, 271; Kathy Hendrickson 266, 267, 276, 281, 282; Jan North 272; Bryna Waldman 280; Susan Dodge 283, 286.

Photographs: All photographs by Silver Burdett & Ginn (SB&G) unless otherwise noted. Table of Contents: Photos; Gene Anthony for SB&G, Scott Clemens/Sand Dollar Photography for SB&G. 4–5: Gene Anthony for SB&G. 8: Scott Clemens/Sand Dollar Photography for SB&G. 9: Gene Anthony for SB&G. 10: M. Timothy O'Keefe/Tom Stack & Associates. 11: Brian Parker/Tom Stack & Associates. 20 *t.l.* Michal Heron; *t.r.* J. Gerard Smith; *t.m.* Tom Stack/Tom Stack & Associates; *b.l.* G. Cloyd/Taurus Photos; *b.r.b.* Michal Heron. 21. *t.l.* Harvey Lloyd/Peter Arnold, Inc.; *b.l.* Jean Claude LeJeune/Stock, Boston; *t.m.* Ward Wells/Shostal/SuperStock; *m.m.* David Stone/Berg & Associates; *b.m.* Michal Heron; *t.r.* Jacques Jangoux/Peter Arnold Inc.; *m.r.* Moos-Hake, Greenberg/Peter Arnold, Inc.; *b.r.* J. Gerard Smith. 25: John Running/Stock, Boston. 33: Gene Anthony for SB&G. 34: *t.l.* Susan Murphy; *b.l.* Bob Daemmrich; *t.r.* Don & Pat Valenti; *m.r.* George Dritsas/Light Images; *b.* Gwen Berghora. 40: Cliff Hollenbeck. 43: Gerhard Gescheidle/Peter Arnold, Inc. 44: *l.* Eve Arnold/Magnum; *m.* Erich Hartmann/Magnum; *r.* Werner Stoy/Camera Hawaii. 46: William Berssenbrugge/Shostal/SuperStock. 47: M. Timmoth O'Keefe/Bruce Coleman Inc. 55: NASA. 61: Scott Clemens/Sand Dollar Photography for SB&G. 66: Phil Datso/Light Images. 67: NASA; *l.* Scott Clemens/Sand Dollar Photography for SB&G. 72: *t.* J. Gerard Smith; *b.* Susan Johns. 73: *t.* Michal Heron; *l.* H. Oizinger/Leo deWys; *r.* Susan Johns. 76: Paul Kuhn/Tom Stack & Associates. 77: Gene Anthony for SB&G; 79: Gene Anthony/Light Images. 80: Harald Sund. 81: © Mickey Jones. 84: Harald Sund. 87: John Sell Cotman, THE MARKETPLACE, Norwich, 1807, Abbot Hall Art Gallery Kendal, England. 88: © 1991 Robert Frerck/Woodfin Camp & Associates. 89: Harald Sund. 89: R. Schmiedt/Leo DeWys, Inc. 90: Gene Anthony for SB&G.; *r.* Scott Clemens/Sand Dollar Photography for SB&G. 91: Scott Clemens/Sand Dollar Photography for SB&G. 108: Scott Clemens/Sand Dollar Photography for SB&G. 109: Gene Anthony for SB&G. 115: Scott Clemens/Sand Dollar Photography for SB&G. 121, 132: Gene Anthony for SB&G. 132: *b.* Scott Clemens/Sand Dollar Photography for SB&G. 133: Gene Anthony for SB&G. 135: Scott Clemens/Sand Dollar Photography for SB&G. 136: Gene Anthony for SB&G. 143: Gene Anthony for SB&G. 144: Kjell B. Sandved 147: Gene Anthony for SB&G. 153: Scott Clemens/Sand Dollar Photography for SB&G. 157: Gene Anthony for SB&G. 160, 161, 175: Gene Anthony for SB&G. 176: Dan DeWilde for SB&G. 207: Gene Anthony for SB&G. 213: © 1991 Eastcott-Momatiak/Woodfin Camp & Associates. 224: © Llewellyn, 225: Arthur Levine/Leo DeWys Inc. 227: Stephen Sutton/Duomo. 240: Michael J. Howell. 240: *b.* Russell Johnson. 250: Scott Clemens/Sand Dollar Photography for SB&G. 253: © Robert Fried/Robert Freid Photography. 265: Michael J. Howell. 265: Greg Gawlowski/Light Images. 284, 285: Gene Anthony for SB&G. 288: Scott Clemens/Sand Dollar Photography for SB&G. 289: Gene Anthony for SB&G. SOUND BANK PHOTOGRAPHS. Silver Burdett & Ginn and John Bacchus, courtesy of Yamaha International Corporation, Buena Park, California; Dorn & Kirschner Band Instrument Co., Union, NJ; and the Morris School District, Board of Education, Morristown, N.J.

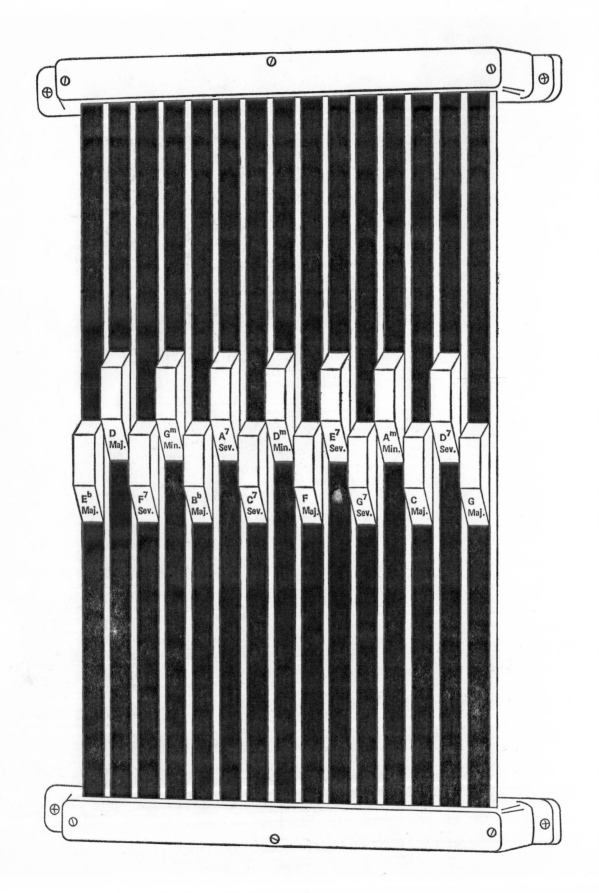